TRAINING WHEELS

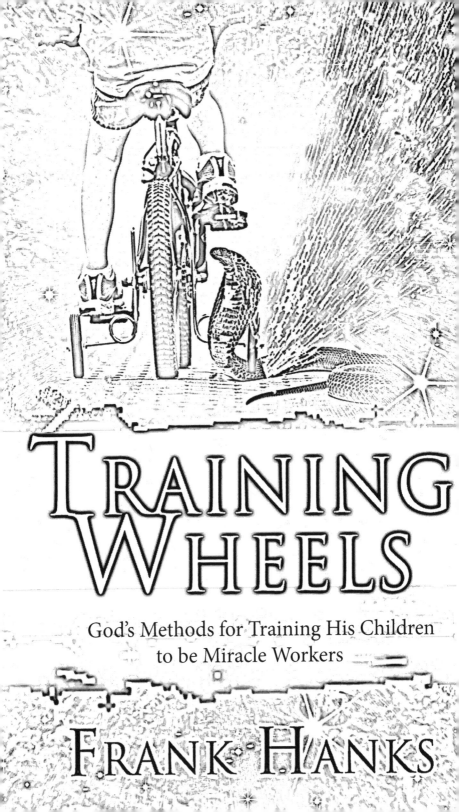

TRAINING WHEELS

God's Methods for Training His Children
to be Miracle Workers

FRANK HANKS

TRAINING WHEELS
by Frank Hanks

Copyright © 2013 by Frank Hanks

Print ISBN: 978-0-9920730-0-8
eBook ISBN: 978-0-9920730-1-5

PUBLISHER CONTACT INFO

E-mail
emptyhospitals@gmail.com.

Website
www.emptyhospitals.org

Mailing Address
Empty Hospitals Publishing
PO Box 28013 Highland Green
Red Deer, AB. T4N 7C2
Canada

All Scripture quotations are taken from the King James Version of the Holy Bible, which is in the public domain.

Empty Hospitals Publishing
The miracle of ink and paper

DEDICATION

I dedicate this book to Betty Cherry. It is Betty who introduced me to the Holy Spirit. She made sure that I knew about
the baptism in the Holy Ghost so that I could receive power
from on high. She instructed me on the purposes of praying
in tongues and abiding in Christ through the anointing of the
Holy Ghost.

With the activation of my prayer language and the subse-
quent surrender to the Holy Spirit, I began to understand what
John was talking about concerning the anointing.

> These things have I written unto you concerning
> them that seduce you. But the anointing which
> ye have received of him abideth in you, and ye
> need not that any man teach you: but as the
> same anointing teacheth you of all things, and
> is truth, and is no lie, and even as it hath taught
> you, ye shall abide in him. (1 John 2:26-27)

My Greatest need was not to be instructed by men, but it
was to be instructed by the Holy Ghost. Without Betty's timely
intervention in my Life, I might have wandered for years without getting to know the great and mighty Holy Ghost

> But ye have an unction from the Holy One, and
> ye know all things. (1 John 2:20)

Thanks, Betty.

PREFACE

From my first days as a Christian, I was drawn to the works that Jesus did. I read many books that spoke of healing and told of the great healing evangelists following World War II such as Jack Coe, A.A. Allen, and Oral Roberts. I studied the gifts of the spirit, believing that they were for everyone who had been baptized in the Holy Spirit. In these studies, I learned about ministers who had performed special miracles. Some were especially gifted, even healing others of heart conditions or getting people out of wheelchairs. Deep in my heart, I cried out to God, hoping that He would bless me in a similar way.

> But covet earnestly the best gifts: and yet shew
> I unto you a more excellent way (1 Corinthians
> 12:31).

I thought about healing all the time. Out of a very full heart, I taught others what I had learned and even went to the hospital to pray for the sick. Although I was trying, I didn't see very many results, and I did not lead anyone to Christ for some time.

One summer night, my friends and I were supposed to travel to Knoxville, Tennessee for a church meeting. Somehow, our wires got crossed and they left without me. I decided to drive there myself, even though I didn't know where the church was, trusting that if I went to Knoxville, the Lord would guide me to where they were. On the way there I saw a gospel tent on the grounds of an Assemblies of God Church. The moment I saw it I just knew that I was supposed to go to their meeting instead. Being there felt wonderful. The tent was full and all the people worshipped, entering into the presence of God together. Then the visiting Prophet came to the microphone. He spoke for a while. Stopped. He called out to me saying, "Young man, please stand up." Once I was sure he meant me, I stood. He prophesied.

He told me that God was very pleased with my decision to clean up my life and follow Him. He said that God had seen my unsuccessful attempts to win the lost, and that He would teach me how to get through to them. He said God would give me a ministry like that of Joshua, and I would lead people. He said that no man would ever be able to stand against me, for God would be with me. He told me to be strong and of good courage and not to turn to the right or left, but to keep going straight.

I was speechless. No one at the meeting knew me, much less this man, yet the words he spoke resonated with my heart and my walk with God. They were accurate. That night, excitement kept me from sleep. I read the book of Joshua several times, anticipating God's instruction on how to win the lost and wondering what God had meant.

After a few weeks and several more unsuccessful attempts to heal the sick, Betty Cherry and another friend of mine went to an all-black church in Atlanta where Betty's husband was invited to preach. The church's pastor was a well-dressed black woman who possessed an unusual grace; she seemed to know exactly what to say when she spoke and it was obvious that everyone respected her. She took the microphone, intending to introduce her guest speaker, but then she called out to me, asking me to stand. I did, and she, too, prophesied over me.

She told me that God was pleased with me and wanted to give me a special gift. She said that somewhere on my body, I would feel extremely hot. This sensation would be a sign to me that the power of the Lord was present to heal. That would be the environment in which I would pray for the sick and they would be healed.

Thrilled, I cried out to God every day for those words to come to pass. I longed to heal the sick.

For most of my days, I immersed myself in the Word of God and in praying in tongues. I would get up at 5:00 a.m. every morning and pray for an hour. Then I would wake up my pastor, and together, we'd pray for at least another hour. I often preached to him, teaching him things I'd learned, some of which found its way into his own messages. After a month or so, the early mornings got to him and he told me I was wearing him out. Knowing he had to find me a new audience for my sermons if he wanted a chance to sleep, he recommended me for a jail ministry. I felt nervous, but I said yes.

Before going to the jail for the first time, I sought the Lord, asking Him to give me a sign that I was really called to preach. I wanted to lead five people to the Lord during our time in the jail. I concluded that if He did not give me that sign, then maybe I was not called. In the Tennessee of the late eighties, jails were the old fashion kind where the cells were all interconnected, and there was a common area at one end for the prisoners to play cards, use the bathroom and hang out. We stood outside the bars, began the service with a few songs, and then my pastor introduced me.

I began my sermon by telling them that I knew what it was like to spend time in jail. I was once locked up for a few days. The worst part of being in jail was the realization that my freedom had been taken away. I could not choose to get out on my own; only the people standing on the other side of the bars could choose to release me. I told them that, while some of them had been there much longer, even months or years, those bars that confine them were nothing compared to the bars around their hearts. The jail they sat in was temporary, but some of them have had the bars around their hearts their whole life. I told them that Christ was on the other side, and He could remove the bars that, for many years, had locked them into routines that caused them to fail again and again.

In 15 minutes, I was finished. Standing there, I had no idea what to do next, so I asked my pastor to take over. He invited those who wished to have the bars removed from their heart to receive Jesus. Six people came forward and received salvation. While they were praying, my right arm started to burn and become hot. I screamed, "The power of the Lord is present to heal. The power of the Lord is present to heal!!!" Everyone looked at me like I was crazy, including my pastor, but I couldn't contain my excitement and asked them if anyone was sick.

They looked at each other for a second or two, and then a young man said he had a sore throat. I told him to step up to the bars because Jesus was going to heal him right then.

The moment those words left my mouth, doubt crept into my mind. I had never said anything so brazen—how would I deal with it if God didn't heal him?

I heard the Holy Spirit ask, "What makes you think I don't want to heal him?"

So I stepped up to the prison bars and prayed for the man. His sore throat went away. Everyone there, including myself, was shocked. I had prayed for many people before but I had never seen an instant healing.

This time was different. This sign was my first introduction to what I now refer to as *spiritual training wheels*. With this gift the Holy Spirit helped me to step out into miracles before I was knowledgeable enough to do so. I believe the Holy Spirit gives these abilities freely, enabling anyone to operate as Jesus did while on the earth.

I was very new in my walk with God and I longed for guidance into spiritual maturity, but few people knew about the gifts of the Holy Spirit or how to receive these gifts. Several people even discouraged me. None of this, however, would stop me. I was determined to go where God was leading.

GIFTS ESTABLISH BELIEVERS

> For I long to see you, that I may impart unto
> you some spiritual gift, *to the end ye may be estab-*
> *lished* (Romans 1:11, Italics mine).

The apostle Paul longed to impart spiritual gifts to the believers in Rome. And in the same way, through the gift of prophecy, the pastor in Atlanta imparted a spiritual gift to me. This gift was meant to establish me, to ensure success while I learned how to minister the gospel. It was like a set of training wheels that allowed me to operate in a realm in which I had a limited amount of experience or knowledge. This is how the Holy Spirit trains people who are serious about doing the works of Christ.

The apostle Paul said that the gifts were designed to *establish* believers.

In his 1828 edition of *The American Dictionary of the English Language*, Noah Webster defines the word "establish" as "[t]o set or fix firmly or unalterably; to settle permanently." Becoming established is meant to be a permanent action; and believers are to be settled in their walk with God by these gifts. The gift God had given me *unalterably, permanently settled the ministry of praying for the sick in my life*. With a single act of His grace God confirmed that I was called and capable of healing the sick. He gave me these training wheels as a foundation to establish me for the works that He has called me to do.

This manifestation has occurred many times since; sometimes it was meant for a single person, and other times for entire rooms of people who were healed at once. These manifestations increased my confidence that God has empowered me to heal others. In practical ways, God established my calling to heal the sick. Praise God.

So if the gifts are meant to establish a believer, it seems very important that believers know about these training wheels and as to how these gifts are imparted?

LAYING ON OF HANDS AND PROPHECY

There are several methods for imparting gifts. In a letter to Timothy the apostle Paul speaks of the method as to how Timothy was given "the gift" that was now "in him."

> Neglect not the gift that is in thee, which was given thee by prophecy, with the laying on of the hands of the presbytery (1 Timothy 4:14).

Timothy received his "gift" through the laying on of hands and through prophecy. In my experience, I received them in the same way. The lady Pastor from Atlanta *spoke about them*, and this made it so. God used her to impart gifts through the vehicle of prophecy. She did not lay hands upon me but simply described the gift, how it would it manifest, and how it would work. When it manifests I am to act upon it. Neglecting it would be to do nothing with the gift. To ignore the unction would be a big mistake and an act of disobedience. The gift is meant to bring healing or deliverance which would be aborted should I choose not to act.

Through the laying on of hands, gifts are imparted all the time. But God gives these gifts not just to me, but to all people. I have often sensed that I should impart the gifts of healing to others. Like those who prophesied to me, I in turn, spoke these gifts into others. When believers understand that they too can spread the gifts that they have received, this impartation is multiplied many times over, and can help many more people in a variety of ways.

I like to pray for people and lay my hands on them. Very often I will sense that God wishes to impart some gift. I will simply speak the impartation making the person aware of the gift. I will instruct them as Paul does here, not to neglect it, but to activate them or stir up the gifts through use. These are ministry gifts that are given to believers for the benefit of others. You may not know you have been called to minister to others in such a way, but I assure you, God has assignments and gifts for anyone who will desire them.

I try to work with those believers who receive an impartation right away. In Nigeria in 2010 Scot Murray and I ministered in a setting where 25 widows had gathered. Before the meeting the ministry gave us the file of each widow. The files contained information about each woman such as the number of children they had and other details. They had each written in their files what they wanted in life. Many of them said they wanted business opportunities or education for their children. Widows have it rough in a land where there are no social services. They have to pay for their child's schooling and medical treatment otherwise they forfeit getting an education or may die if the funds are not available to receive medical treatment. Many children die from very treatable illnesses simply because they do not have the money to take their babies to the doctor. It is shocking that this is reality in many places.

We spoke to the women for a few minutes and then told them we would call them one at a time for prayer. We asked them to think about what they wanted to ask God for and that we would pray and God would grant their request. We also told them that we would ask God what He wanted to do for each of them and see what He had to say. The stage was set. We called up a young widow named Angelina.

We prayed for her according to her desires and then we waited to see what God had to say. We heard God calling her to be a leader in her community and especially among the other widows. He also wanted to impart to her gifts of healings and working of miracles. She returned to her seat and we continued to call the other widows and prayed with them one by one. We noticed some of them were sick, so we asked Angelina to come up and help us to pray for the sick. She was delighted. Many widows burdened with sickness came up for prayer.

We taught Angelina how to use her authority to command diseases to leave peoples' bodies. She laid hands on them and every one, without exception, was healed instantly. Praise God! It really is just that simple.

Once again Jesus was true to His leadings. Angelina left that day, established in her ministry of bringing healing to others. She was given lots of opportunities, not only that day, but also in her community delivering others from sickness. She will never forget the training wheels she received that day. The experience of seeing Jesus heal the sick grounded her firmly in doing the works of Christ. Jesus called many of these women that day to do similar things and many gifts were imparted. It was so much fun to be a part of these supernatural impartations that nobody wanted to leave the meeting that day. But what do you do when you run out of sick people to pray for?

I guess that had the thought entered our minds, we might have taken to the streets that day and just healed people for the rest of the day. Maybe next time we will. Or we could have spent the rest of the day at the hospital healing the sick and raising the dead...next time we will. Praise God, for the simplicity of the Kingdom. Anyone can do the works of God if only they believe. It is that simple.

Another way that the anointing for miracles is passed is through garments.

Elijah's cloak or garment was dropped when he was taken to heaven on the chariot of fire.

> And it came to pass, as they still went on, and talked, that, behold, *there appeared* a chariot of fire, and horses of fire, and parted them both asunder; and Elijah went up by a whirlwind into heaven. And Elisha saw *it,* and he cried my

father, my father, the chariot of Israel, and the horsemen thereof. And he saw him no more: and he took hold of his own clothes, and rent them in two pieces. He took up also the mantle of Elijah that fell from him, and went back, and stood by the bank of Jordan; and he took the mantle of Elijah that fell from him, and smote the waters, and said, where *is* the LORD God of Elijah? And when he also had smitten the waters, they parted hither and thither: and Elisha went over (2 Kings 2:11–14).

The chariot drove right between them and Elisha was left standing on the ground while Elijah was swept away into the chariot. The good news was that Elijah's mantle that was left on the ground was the same one that Elisha took and used to part the waters. Notice that Elisha took off the garments he was wearing and ripped them. He did not want to walk in his own strength when he could walk in the mighty anointing of his master. He was ready for the double portion anointing that Elijah said he would get if he saw him leave the earth. He had the understanding that Elijah's mantle was left behind for a reason.

A DOUBLE PORTION OF CHRIST'S MANTLE . . . ANYONE INTERESTED?

And while they looked stedfastly toward heaven as he went up, behold, two men stood by them in white apparel; Which also said, Ye men of Galilee, why stand ye gazing up into heaven? this same Jesus, which is taken up from you into heaven, shall so come in like manner as ye have seen him go into heaven (Acts 1:10–11).

I wonder if the angels' question had to do with a double portion anointing that would be left for Christ's new creation? Notice how Elisha immediately ripped his clothes and grabbed the double portion held in the mantle of Elijah, but the disciples just stood there gazing. Just as Elisha saw Elijah, when he was taken up, so the apostles saw Jesus when he was taken up. I believe that the double portion anointing is foundational for equipping us to do the works of Christ and greater.

I would like the double portion of Jesus's anointing, how about you? Let's rip off our old rags of religion and grab His righteous, holy garments. I believe that we can do greater works than He did. After all, Elisha has twice as many miracles recorded than his predecessor Elijah. Why not believe to perform twice as many miracles as Jesus?

While on a trip to Africa, a man approached the manager of the motel where we were staying, and asked him if he could buy the sheets from my hotel bed. He wanted to wrap himself in them because he wanted a transference of the anointing he noticed in me. Sounds funny if you think about it; but maybe he was hoping for something from God that he felt would come through a transference of anointing held in the fabric. I never heard whether he was successful to buy them. But I admire his hunger. It is a hunger rarely seen in North America.

The Mantle is Real

I was visiting some friends one day. We worshipped the Lord for quite a while with music and prayer. Afterwards a young prophet said that God instructed him to "throw his coat upon each of us." We agreed and he went around the room dropping his coat over our shoulders. When he dropped it on me, I felt warmth and energy pass through me. I also smelled and tasted oil. My skin and hair became oily and I felt as though I was filling up with oil on the inside. A saturation of this anointing permeated my entire being, bringing a peace that I had never known.

After this encounter I began to prophecy into the lives of those around me in greater measure. It was only a coat, made of materials found in any other coat, but the reality of the moment was found in what God was accomplishing in each of us as we had the coat on us. This anointing has remained with me for years and is still a part of me. I thank God for all the times, where, as His children, we dare to believe that He wants to improve us, establish us and settle us in His ways and in our particular uniqueness of gifts and callings. What a blessing it is to walk with God.

On several occasions, God has instructed me to throw my coat on others. Each time dramatic transfers take place. The person receiving always knew that God was doing something very special. Just as God used a cloak to transfer the mantle from Elijah to Elisha we learn that this is a scriptural method of transference or impartation of spiritual gifts to establish us in the faith. The coat was a point of contact and a physical reminder of what God is doing in and through each of us.

There were also gifts imparted to me that I didn't even realize I had received. Somehow they were imparted in a manner unknown or hidden at the time, but I began operating in other gifts as the Spirit of God moved upon me. I like to believe that praying in other tongues directed me into many of these encounters. I have always been spiritually keen and I attribute this to continual prayer. Engaging in prayer positions you for greatness. Time and again I find myself imparting gifts to others in the same ways I have received them.

ADDICTED TO MINISTRY

Greatness is to serve as many people as you can with what God has given you. The greatest of all is the servant. A great believer is one who has become addicted to serving the saints.

Watch ye, stand fast in the faith, quit you like men, be strong. Let all your things be done with charity. I beseech you, brethren, (ye know the house of Stephanas, that it is the firstfruits of Achaia, and *that* they have addicted themselves to the ministry of the saints) (1 Corinthians 16:13–15).

The members of the house of Stephanas were great believers and had addicted themselves to the ministry of the saints. In my mind, they built their entire reason for living around ministering to the saints. This seems a great honor to me. Imagine using your whole life to assist and build up others. We can all include these sacred acts into our daily routines. We can all impart to others; impacting them and inspiring them to do the works of Christ. It would be just like taking a few minutes of your time to help your child put training wheels on their bicycle...you would do that, wouldn't you?

My greatest joy comes in seeing others do the works of Christ for the first time. I get to see the wonder and awe written on their faces as they watch a miracle take place. I love to get new believers and activate them right away to receive the gifts and use them. It is a great experience that never gets old. God is always so faithful to work with anyone who will train others to do what He has established in them. Thank you Jesus!

WHO LIKES STEW?

We were hosting a prophet from Malaysia, brother Mathew Nuek (I love you Mathew) for several weeks in 2011. During this time God used us to minister to this wonderful man of God and he also ministered to us. One day a thought came into my mind of how great stew tastes when it has been slow cooking for hours. As the thought came I told the others about it. Then God said He wanted to make a stew.

When making a stew you gather all the spices, vegetables, and meats. On its own each ingredient has its own flavor. But what makes a stew taste so good is that while it is simmering in the pot, the individual flavors mingle and over the hours of cooking the separate ingredients become a wonderful and delicious stew. As I explained this process to them, we realized that God was suggesting a blending of our gifts and anointing. We prayed for the transference and blending of the gifts into each of us so that we would carry new gifts and anointing.

As we prayed we believed that God was doing something very special. The result was that each of us now carried some new empowerment. Our prophet friend, Brother Mathew, who was with us on a mission to the aboriginal peoples of Canada, experienced a dramatic increase in gifts of healings, gifts of working of miracles, and the gift of faith. God is so very cool. We trust God to do whatever He has in mind for us. He never disappoints. I look forward to ministering with Brother Mathew in his native Malaysia in 2013 God willing.

Because of these impartations and a willingness to get my hands dirty, bodies are healed, people are born again, and others have found that their desire to serve God is one act of grace away from fulfillment. They found their training wheels to establish them on the road to the greatest adventure they will ever experience. It reminds me of the joy I experienced when I saw my child take her first steps.

SPECIAL MIRACLES

Two weeks ago, a man I know, gave me a call and said that for the last two weeks he could not quit thinking about me and knew that he had to call me. He invited me to have supper with him at a friend's house where he was house-sitting and caring for his friend's pet while he was on holidays. It was a five million dollar house on many acres of land right at the edge of the city. It was impressive, but I was curious to find out what God's purpose was for this meeting.

The homeowner's elderly mother was also there. After supper we sat in the living room and it became clear that the elder lady had some issues with a couple of churches she had attended. She was carrying some wounds and also struggled with who she was in Christ. There was an internal war raging inside her that was beginning to cause problems with her health. She was showing symptoms of someone about ready to have a stroke.

Once we discovered what the root lies and misunderstandings were, we led her through to the truth with the scriptures. Once she repented of believing the lies and got rid of the inner conflicts, she instantly felt better. When you find out that what you have believed is a lie an interesting thing happens, you realize that you are free to enjoy the truth.

That same night we decided to have a party. Each of us took a bottle of anointing oil and anointed one another and prayed for an impartation - a cross pollination of sorts. While we prayed for each other, words of prophecy were shared, visions were seen and shared, and we were filled to overflowing with the Spirit of God. We glorified God and thanked Him for the fellowship and for the manifestations of the gifts of the Spirit.

We were "in the spirit." The elderly lady then went into another part of the house and returned with a bolt of fabric. It was a quilt of squares each of which had a picture of Jesus on the cross with a caption beneath Him that said, "I believe in Jesus." She cut out 12 or more squares and said she had the idea that we might each anoint the blocks with the same oil that each of us had used to anointing each other. There were 4 of us, so we each anointed every square in the same spot so that the fragrance of all four oils would be in the cloth.

According to her, the purpose of anointing the squares was so that we could take the cloths to different parts of the world. She recited a list of the nations where these squares would be sent. I like doing these kinds of acts, to not only memorialize time spent together, but also to release the anointing of God for others. When I consider that I am God's child, to me it is as though our Father is coming to play with us. When He plays with us our imagination is fertile. I totally believe that simple, silly acts like this one are breathed on by God, and that He will use these cloths to do miracles.

I took about eight of them with me because I will travel to Malaysia and Africa this year. I intend to give them out to people who need a miracle of healing or deliverance.

> And God wrought special miracles by the hands of Paul: So that from his body were brought unto the sick handkerchiefs or aprons, and the diseases departed from them, and the evil spirits went out of them (Acts 19:11–12).

Paul said something that has stuck with me for some time now.

> Those things, which ye have both learned, and received, and heard, and seen in me, do: and the God of peace shall be with you (Philippians 4:9).

THOSE THINGS

. . . He said whatever I have both learned and received and hear and seen in Him, as I do them, the God of peace shall be with me.

Already there has been some blessing from distributing the anointed squares. I gave the first one to a lady I led to the Lord who is now skipping grades in the Spirit realm. She is so hungry to get to know Jesus. She was deeply touched because she had nothing in her house with the words, "I believe in Jesus" written on it. That night I laid hands upon her and prayed. The same presence and sense of wholeness from the night we anointed the cloths completely filled her heart and home that night. Her face looked as though 10 years had come off her. She was radiant and glowing. God came to play with us and bless us again. The God of all peace, decided to show up again. It is interesting how He shows up whenever and where ever He is invited, isn't it?

A day later I picked up a couple of these squares and smelled the beautiful fragrances of the blended oils. I like smelling them and remembering that night again. I remember thinking that I would like to smell them while writing so I put one on each shoulder and sat down at my computer to work on this book. You know what happened? The same fullness of the Spirit we enjoyed that night visited me again at my keyboard. I was instantly in the spirit. The God of all peace settled afresh upon me.

It is interesting that just telling the story brings the same manifestation again. There He is again. He is settling upon you even as you read this. I believe that you too will have the impartation just by reading about it.

Do it Father. Bring a deep abiding anointing to the heart of everyone who reads this book and into every home this book enters. Just like when you blessed the house of Obededom the Gittite (2 Samuel. 6:10–12) when the ark visited his home, in Jesus Name, Amen! Impart to every reader the grace to be changed and cross-pollinate us in Christ. Bring a oneness and a strengthening of our love for each other.

I fully expect many breakthroughs in the nations as these cloths go into them. I fully expect a breakout of unusual miracles. This book will come off the press right before our trip to Malaysia. Many will read it and as they read they will witness and receive the miracles that we prophecy about today. \o/ praise the Lord!

Thank you Lord for your special miracle outbreak birthed from this time of fellowship with my friends. Reward this lady who had it in her heart to do this with the cloths. Also Father, inspire others to dream with You, play with You and heal with You. We are all able to do these kinds of prophetic acts. Assure everyone who reads this book that you have left no one out of the party…everyone is invited to dream with You and bravely step out to bring Your miracle working power in the simplest expressions of faith. May many come to know You and be blessed as they enter into and participate in the prophetic acts that You lay on their hearts to perform. Father, glorify Your Son Jesus as we ask You in His name.

CONTENTS

INTRODUCTION

B icycles come in many shapes and sizes. There are bicycles for every age group and every skill level. The tricycle is for the littlest people who are unable to balance a two wheel bike on their own and may get injured trying because they are not developed enough. It can be scary to go from a trike to a bike with two wheels.

Back when I was a kid there were no bike helmets or padding that you wore to lessen the shock and the pain of falling off your bike or running into a tree. We just jumped on the bike and, by trial and error, through much tribulation, learned to ride a bike. During the earliest stages of learning, I remember wrecking many times until I had mastered the bicycle. Crashing was not a question of if, but when. Getting hurt was much the same: not if, but when and how bad. As a kid, I wanted to do everything, and the pain of crashing seemed somehow worth the liberty and fun of riding my own bike without the assistance of others. Provided you keep trying, there comes a day when you are good at riding a bike.

Training wheels are wheels that you attach to the back tire of the bike to keep it upright so that someone who has not yet learned to balance a bike may ride and get the feel of riding a bike while protecting the rider from some of the pain of learning, but also enabling the little one to operate above their current skill level or understanding. This book will help you do the same and establish you as you continue to learn by actively doing.

This is only one example of the many aids available to us to assist in our development, but it is a good model for understanding how our Father supports our learning and insures our success. Using age appropriate methods is something the Father has accounted for in your training. Spiritual training wheels are available to those who wish to operate as He does, even before you feel qualified to do so. The Holy Spirit is an expert at equipping anyone who is willing to learn.

This is the Idea that will help us to see how God supports us as we learn to operate just like Jesus.

To do the works of Christ consistently it is important that you become an environment for sustainable breakthrough. Spiritual training wheels are a skill-set of core competencies and empowerment from the Holy Spirit, enabling any believer to operate as Christ before they are experienced enough to do so. The Holy Spirit wants to equip you with heaven's competencies as you discover the inborn aptitudes you have inherited as a son or daughter of God.

You may think it is unreasonable to expect that you are capable of operating like Jesus, but I promise you, Jesus believes that you can. He believes in us and our abilities long before we are confident in performing them; after all, He is the Author of them. He trusted that 12 ordinary men, His disciples would be able to do the same works that He did. These disciples are not in the world anymore, yet you and I are His present day disciples.

> *You can and will do the works of Christ.*

Back in the early days of my training, I witnessed believers who were healing the sick. Before my eyes I watched as blind eyes were opened, deaf people heard for the first time and people who were sick or diseased found freedom. As I watched, I wondered if the people performing these miracles were somehow more gifted or special than I. Jesus would say to me "You can do that." I thought I was imagining this voice. I remember reasoning that I could not do these things, but deep inside I wanted to do so, just as much as I wished to ride a bike "like the big boys" before I learned how.

I searched the scriptures and noticed the frustration Jesus must have had bringing the disciples to the place that they believed they could do the same things He did. You can tell that they were deeply moved by witnessing the miracles which He did and the wisdom of the words He spoke. He could do anything. They wanted to do the same works He did.

They weren't the only ones who wanted to do the works of God. He was asked one day "what must we do that we might work the works of God." Jesus responded by saying "this is the work of God; that you believe on the one whom he has sent (John 6:28–29)

This is surprisingly similar to John 14:12:

> Verily, verily, I say unto you, he that *believeth on me*, the works that I do shall he do also; and greater works than these shall he do; because I go unto my Father.

The prerequisite to doing the works He did is to believe on Him. With God nothing is impossible. And, nothing shall be impossible to Him that believeth. Nothing is impossible for God, and nothing is impossible for you if you believe. Both statements are true. Believing in Him makes all things possible for you and me. Yes, I am talking about you.

And Jesus said unto them, Because of your unbelief: for verily I say unto you, If ye have faith as a grain of mustard seed, ye shall say unto this mountain, Remove hence to yonder place; and it shall remove; and *nothing shall be impossible unto you* (Matthew 17:20, italics mine).

> For with God *nothing shall be impossible* (Luke 1:37, italics mine).

Believing is essential for anyone wanting to do the works of God. Many people claim to believe but when you bring up the subject of doing the works of Christ few have a working knowledge. There is an old saying that comes to mind: those who can, do, and those who cannot, teach. If knowledge without application were sufficient, this would make sense. However In the kingdom of God such a statement is tragic. Those who teach should be the ones who best model the works of Christ for us. As we move towards the model that Jesus used, we can rid ourselves of such notions and be doers of the word.

WORDS WITHOUT ACTION FALL SHORT OF THE GLORY OF GOD.

> The former treatise have I made, O Theophilus, of all that Jesus began both to *do and teach*, Until the day in which he was taken up, after that he through the Holy Ghost had given commandments unto the apostles whom he had chosen (Acts 1:1–3 Italics mine).

Luke thought it was important to lay out "all that Jesus began both to do and teach." Doing and teaching go hand in hand. Teaching without action lacks credibility, and learning without doing is incomplete. Would a teacher who is not doing what he is teaching be classified as one who believes?

Deciding to learn what it takes to truly believe is at the heart of the matter.

Desire will compel us to take whatever *action* is needed to complete our goal. Action? Yes action! Like with the bicycle, action must be taken. Children desire adventure, wanting to try everything, action is very natural to a child.

It is only a matter of time before a child is doing or taking the action required to learn.

This developmental process is hardwired into the child. The kingdom of God emphasizes taking responsibility, which is evidenced by not only hearing, but also by doing the word of God. **Demonstration of kingdom power is lacking.** Signs follow those who believe (Mark 16:17). The word "follow" suggests that these signs are only present when we are moving.

Get a group of kids together and suggest that they are able to perform miracles and the dynamics change dramatically. The atmosphere becomes charged with expectancy and a desire for someone to model it for them, and help them to connect with Jesus, and tell them that all they need to do to perform miracles is to believe.

Once this fundamental understanding comes, faith is released and children want to get busy healing the sick. Children naturally utilize gifts of the Holy Ghost. Tell them what it is for and how to use it and they want to do it. An adult might ask God to bless someone or heal someone, but a child may just ask God to show them how they can do it.

Children are powerful ministers because they have not yet been taught unbelief. Neither do they think that we should all just wait on God to perform the miracles. They rarely fall short of the glory of God unless someone comes along and "straightens them out" with a proper dose of unbelief.

An example of falling short of the glory is a belief system that stops "at what God can do" but fails to acknowledge our part in doing what He said we could if we believed.

No one would dispute that God can do anything; He can speak to the weather, open the eyes of the blind, heal the sick, cast out devils, and even raise the dead. Yet, most people are totally without an answer when someone suggests that they, too, are able to do such exploits.

I have often thought that we hide behind the false disclaimer that "we are unable to heal anyone." This takes the responsibility off us and places it solely upon God, who, incidentally, placed the responsibility upon us. He said, "As long as I am in the world, I am the light of the world" (John 9:5). However, before He ascended into heaven He told His disciples "ye are the light of the world" and that their light should not be hidden but placed upon a candlestick so that it may give light to all that are in the house (Matthew 5:14). He healed the sick and then He told his disciples to heal the sick. He cast out devils then sent his disciples out, who were astonished that devils were subject to them, just like they were to Christ (Luke 10:17).

A disciple is anyone who is following Christ. Jesus was training His disciples to do the very same works He did. This is very clear throughout the four gospels. There were many disciples beside the twelve He chose initially. The principle of following Him and doing the works that He did continues to this day. As His disciple you are capable of doing the same acts.

He empowers us just like He empowered them and sends us just like He sent them. We are able to do what He did and greater because He has gone to the Father and sent the Holy Spirit to us. (see John 14:12). Currently, all power in heaven and earth are His, it is in all power, that we go in His name. That name carries all power in heaven and in earth (Matthew 28:18). How much power do you need to heal cancer? Surely you would not need "all power." However, if it required all power, it would be at your disposal if you believe.

Training wheels supply the support to establish you in riding a bike, just as all power is enough to establish you in your calling of doing the works of Christ.

1

THE FILING SYSTEM

Trust in the LORD with all thine heart; and lean not unto thine own understanding In all thy ways acknowledge him, and he shall direct thy paths (Proverbs 3:5).

God has a family. This family exists in both heaven and in earth. They are called by His name and have answered the call to be born again. The family has a different way of approaching reality; a better way. We are to acknowledge our Lord in all that we do, knowing that He will direct our paths, not leaning on our own understanding but trusting in Him with all of our hearts.

What makes God's way of doing things better than what we think?

OUR UNDERSTANDING

From the moment you were born into this world you started to become familiar with everything about it. Through your physical body you touch the physical world, through the intellect and soul you touch the intellectual and emotional realm. Now through the new birth, you have been recreated in Christ Jesus. You have a new spirit that is created perfect.

As a new creation God has equipped us more perfectly in that we are not mere men and women anymore but have been made partakers of His divine nature through a new birth. Through our regenerated spirit, we are able to touch the spiritual realm; we have gained access to a realm invisible to us previously, but now it is being revealed to us by the Spirit of God.

God is a Spirit, and provided you have been born again, your spirit is made alive with God. You are now gaining new data from a previously unseen realm. Just as when you were born as a baby, you are again learning to live as the new creation you have become. An invisible kingdom, not previously known by sight, nor imagined in your heart, is being made known to you.

> But as it is written, Eye hath not seen, nor ear heard, neither have entered into the heart of man, the things which God hath prepared for them that love him. But God hath revealed them unto us by his Spirit: for the Spirit searcheth all things, yea, the deep things of God. For what man knoweth the things of a man, save the spirit of man which is in him? even so the things of God knoweth no man, but the Spirit of God (1 Corinthians 2:9 - 11).

Now that you have come into this kingdom, instead of using your five physical senses to explore this kingdom you will now learn to trust more in an invisible spectrum of reality. Much like a baby cannot know what is beyond the womb unless she first is delivered from it, this spectrum is unknown to you until you are born into it. You now have come forth into a new reality having been delivered into it through the new birth.

Now you are able to explore this new realm. You are learning its protocol, but you are learning it not as the old man who was dead indeed in trespasses and sin, but as the new man who has passed from death unto life (see Ephesians 2:11 & John3:14). Your spirit, now alive to God, is capable of learning a new way of living and interacting with the world.

Consider all the retained memory, including data stored from life experience gathered from birth till now, our conscious mind works with the unconscious mind sorting through multiple combinations of choices available to you based upon past experiences, education, emotions, fears successes and failures. The data is almost endless.

This data and our relationship to knowing it, using it or fearing it, is all part of our natural understanding.

Think of yourself as a very complex office, the control center of a life. In the office you have billions of filing cabinets, each labeled differently. When you hear the word, Catholic for example, your mind retrieves the file labeled Catholic. Each of us would be able to talk about this subject till we have exhausted the file. Many of us could speak for hours, not only about the Catholic Church, but also the numerous encounters of people who are Catholic.

Another file is labeled mother. It has incalculable data on motherhood, my mother, other mothers, what makes a good mother, example of bad mothers, what mother likes, dislikes, will not allow. We can see her smile, feel her touch and hear her voice. Our experiences with our mothers might teach us that mothers are supposed to be nurturing, loving and kind. We learn that mother is the one to whom we run when we fall and scrape our knee. Or perhaps our experience has taught us that mothers are moody, emotionally unavailable and harsh. The slightest change in the sound of her voice or one of her looks and we know her mood is changed. She may have beaten you, spoken horribly to you, comforted you, encouraged you or hurt you. You learned what not to do around her for fear of being punished. You knew all her rules. When mother was around you learned that you had to navigate emotional landmines.

How about the multitudes of people that you meet? We soon realize that some people are friendly and others not. Each individual has their unique experiences, rules, pains, traumas, joys, sins. It is mind boggling the multi-faceted complexity of operations.

These files form part of our **understanding** concerning any subject. It is our own understanding, exclusive to us as individuals. If you wish to know what's in a person's filing system, just bring up a subject and within seconds, as the man or woman engages the retrieval system directly tied to their mouths, your education as to who they are begins. For the next hour they could speak non-stop. I know I can.

Is our understanding complete? No. Are our files dependable? Sometimes, but at best our information is incomplete. Compared with God's understanding, we know very little.

Now add to these files, data that has been collected from our experiences with of pain, trauma, fear, sin, etc. and the files can be corrupted or inaccessible.

When faced with a particular situation or person, we will draw from these files and make rational or irrational decisions based on these files. Within split seconds, often without being aware of how we arrive at certain conclusions, we form a conscious decision about what to do. A familiar song, or the smell of a certain perfume can trigger responses of nostalgia or sorrow that on the surface, seem inexplicable. We spend our entire human experience gleaning from these pertinent files. These unconscious responses to others and life itself transpire outside of conscious awareness.

As new creations in Christ we are taught *not to lean* on our own understanding. To lean on something means to rest upon, rely upon or have confidence in it. If the files of self and the world around me are corrupted, unreliable or incomplete; to lean *solely upon them* would put me at a disadvantage, and lead me to draw wrong conclusions which when acted upon could be troublesome. Unfortunately, we often believe our conclusions are trustworthy when they may not be.

It is like following a recipe that was written down wrong. You prepare the dish and present it to your hungry guests anticipating that they will enjoy it. Instead when they eat it, frowns appear round the table. Thinking you somehow made a mistake, you attempt to make the same recipe and again you receive the same round of frowns. After a while, if you are wise, you just stop using that recipe. But many of us, given the same choices, will repeat the same mistakes over and over. Somehow, due to corrupted data, our repetitive choices seem to be the only ones to make, even after having the same results every time. This dysfunction is a result of doing what **we know** *to do* based upon incomplete or corrupted data. When our perceptions are formed using incomplete or corrupted data, and we believe them to be true, we are functioning with limited vision, knowledge and wisdom.

> For now we see through a glass darkly; but then face to face: now I know in part; but then shall I know even as also I am known (1 Corinthians 13:12).

If you have ever seen a windshield on a car that has been shattered but still in one piece, it is almost impossible to drive that car. If you did try, you will have to drive slowly and carefully. To go fast would increase your chances of causing an accident or driving off into the ditch. Why? Because you cannot see out of this windshield, the fractured glass causes distorted vision. The windshield is unreliable. You cannot trust it; rely upon it. You must get your windshield fixed if you wish to drive safely.

Relying upon our own understanding is very much like driving the car with the fractured windshield. We are at the mercy of an unreliable product that distorts our vision. This is not to say that we make bad decisions continually. But to rely on our perceptions from files that cause us undue pain, or that are unknowingly jaded and incorrect, without acknowledging that God may have a better plan, is sure to land us in trouble.

Learning a new way to live is part of the introduction into the family of God. But what about the dysfunctional office with the corrupted files, can they be healed; can my soul, which encompass the mind, will and emotions, be restored?

Restoring the Soul

He restoreth my soul: he leadeth me in the paths of righteousness for his name's sake (Psalm 23:3).

The pattern for redeeming or restoring the soul is very simple.

The entrance of thy words giveth light; it giveth understanding unto the simple (Psalm 119:130).

The word of God is the answer to the fractured soul and is the beginning of its sanctification process.

Wherefore lay apart all filthiness and superfluity of naughtiness, and receive with meekness

> the engrafted word, which is able to save your
> souls (James 1:21).

The word of God is engrafted into the heart and when it takes root it products change and healing. As we are healed and transformed we are able to see our life for what it was and we are able to relinquish long held, outdated belief systems and patterns of interacting with our world.

God has new ways of doing things for us to discover and explore. It is imperative that we learn the ways of God from the Spirit of God. When we do, our vision improves; we make better choices because we have tapped into a much superior data. The beauty of leaning on God is that He knows all things including my future. Participation in the transformation process guarantees that your soul will be restored.

> And many people shall go and say, Come ye,
> and let us go up to the mountain of the LORD, to
> the house of the God of Jacob; and *he will teach
> us of his ways*, and we will walk in his paths: for
> out of Zion shall go forth the law, and the word
> of the LORD from Jerusalem (Isaiah 2:3; italics
> mine).

The Three Control Centers

The head office, the brain, is only a part of our complex intelligence or control center. We have a physical heart which, *recent research has shown, is able to make decisions* and choose its own responses.

> Peace I leave with you, my peace I give to you:
> not as the world giveth, give I to you. Let not

your heart be troubled, neither let it be afraid
(John 14:27).

For as he thinketh in his heart, so is he . . .
(Proverbs 23:7a).

. . . that thou mightest know the thoughts of thy
heart (Daniel 2:30).

. . . the thought of thine heart may be forgiven
thee (Acts 8:22b).

Jesus told us not to let our hearts be troubled. This suggests
that we have the ability within the heart to make decisions. To
believe from the heart and to forgive from the heart are Biblical
precepts whose theme can be found throughout the Bible.

Much has been learned about the heart in recent years
since the advent of the heart transplant. Heart transplant recipients report personality changes, memories that belonged to
the donor surfacing in dreams and desires of many kinds for
foods, musical tastes and the list goes on.

From an article titled "Do Hearts Have Memories?
Transplant Patient Gets Craving for Food Eaten by Organ
Donor," Richard Shears writes:

> Before being given the heart of 18-year-old
> Kaden Delaney, who was left brain dead after a
> car crash, Mr. Waters, 24, had 'no desire at all' for
> Burger Rings, ring-shaped hamburger-flavoured
> crisps. [As a direct result of this operation,] [h]e
> now craves Burger Rings--one of Kaden's favorite
> snacks. . . .
>
> The case in Australia adds weight to a theory
> that the brain is not the only organ to store mem-
> ories or personality traits.

Scientists say there are at least 70 document-
ed cases of transplant patients having personality
changes which reflect the characteristics of their
donor.

In an article entitled "Man Given Heart of Suicide Victim
Marries Donor's Widow and Then Kills Himself in Exactly the
Same Way," Paul Thompson writes:

> Another astonishing example is the case of Amer-
> ican Sonny Graham, who received the heart of
> Terry Cottle, who had shot himself in the head.
> After the transplant in 1995 Mr Graham met Mr
> Cottle's widow Cheryl, fell in love and married
> her. Twelve years later Mr Graham picked up a
> gun and shot himself in the throat, leaving Cheryl
> a widow for the second time grieving for two hus-
> bands who had shared a heart.

From the article entitled "Yes, the Heart Really Can
'Think' and Have Emotions! Amazing New Scientific Evidence
Corroborates Biblical Teaching Yet Again!" by Robin A. Brace,
2006 the work of Dr. Andrew Armour is highlighted:

Completely independently of such heart transplant experiences, Dr. Andrew Armour Ph.D. is a heart specialist who
had noticed the presence of neurons in the heart—he noted
a sophisticated collection of these and learned that the heart
contains a complex nervous system of its own. He soon realized
that there is a more intimate connection between the heart and
brain than had previously been known or understood. Indeed,
the doctor claims that the heart actually sends more information to the brain than the other way around! Dr. Armour
has written a pamphlet called, *Anatomical and Functional
Principles*. His publisher makes the following comment about
this writing:

Groundbreaking research in the field of neurocardiology has established that the heart is a sensory organ and a sophisticated information encoding and processing center, with an extensive intrinsic nervous system sufficiently sophisticated to qualify as a "heart brain." Armour discusses intriguing data documenting the complex neuronal processing and memory capabilities of the intrinsic cardiac nervous system, indicating that the heart brain can process information and make decisions about its control independent of the central nervous system. By providing an understanding of the elaborate anatomy and physiology of the cardiac nervous system, this monograph contributes to the newly emerging view of the heart as a complex, self-organized system that maintains a continuous two-way dialogue with the brain and the rest of the body.

The heart governs so many functions in our body and the heart creates perceptions. Our perceptions create our reality. So our understanding is more complex than just what we intellectually have learned, in that our emotions and our will are part of it also.

The gut has not historically been thought of as a storage place for memories, nor has it been thought of as a dwelling place of emotions, but this belief is changing.

All of the experiences of life have an effect on our memories and how we process and store information. The Bible speaks of each of these three control centers of the body.

Our thoughts are a major subject of which God has a lot to say.

The word *heart* is used in the Bible 833 times.

Gut, bowels, belly, innermost parts of the belly, are all mentioned in scripture.

Normally we would not think of the gut as a source for decision-making. Yet, people often have uneasy feelings in their guts when contemplating a bad decision. Some people say, "I had a gut feeling" or "I just went with my gut." The term "gut wrenching" has a connotation of being painfully conflicted. Anxiety and fear causes discomfort in the stomach. People who suffer from anxiety disorders or depression often suffer from digestive problems such as irritable bowel syndrome.

The Bible speaks of the belly as a fountain from which rivers of living water proceed.

> He that believeth on me, as the scripture hath said, out of his belly shall flow rivers of living water (John 7:38).

From my own belly rivers of living water will flow. But in the Book of Proverbs the Bible says that my spirit is the candle of the Lord searching all the inward parts of the belly.

> The spirit of man is the candle of the LORD, searching all the inward parts of the belly (Proverbs 20:27).

My spirit is searching all the inward parts of my belly. What is it searching for and why? What would it find of any use to God if my belly was strictly for digestion and elimination of waste? It seems to me that living water would have a functional purpose. It would generate life. And what would be the result if my belly were wounded? If my innermost parts have been fractured or traumatized it might hinder my life to some degree.

> The words of a talebearer are as wounds, and they go down into the innermost parts of the belly (Proverbs 26:22).

Words have a wounding effect on the innermost parts of the belly. Damage done by words, wounds inflicted that specifically harm the innermost parts of the belly, from which rivers of living water are supposed to flow can be disabling and restrict the life-flow produced in this physical location of the belly. This life-flow is not only a source of life and well being within the person but a source of healing for the benefit of others.

When the Bible talks about restoring the soul, it is referring to healing and delivering us from every destruction and dysfunction that is a result of wounds, trauma, brokenness, weakness, sins or fears. It has to do with all three control centers and more, redeeming your life from what happened in the past.

Since I discovered these findings, and received instruction from the Lord, I have found that my prayers for people have gone much deeper as each of the three areas of the body is included. People claim to be profoundly affected and report an increased sense of peace and well-being. When the wounding experiences and residual memories are healed, physical healing follows quite easily and, at times, suddenly.

Healing people who have been emotionally disabled has long since been a desire of my heart.

When armed with a deeper understanding of what God has to say about our bodies we can approach healing at a neurological level by prayer, eliminating the need for many therapies and drugs that can do more harm than good.

Adam Hadhazy in his article titled "Think Twice: How the Gut's 'Second Brain' Influences Mood and Well-Being—The emerging and surprising view of how the enteric nervous system in our bellies goes far beyond just processing the food we eat," writes:

> A complex, independent nervous system lines the gastrointestinal tract that has been dubbed the "second brain." The enteric nervous system consists of sheaths of neurons in the walls of our

alimentary canal (guts) begins at the esophagus and goes all the way to the anus. Ninety percent of the body's serotonin levels are found there. Serotonin has long been thought to be a contributor to feelings of well-being and happiness.

My belief is that the wounding of the gut brain has resulted in many emotional disorders. These gut brain wounds often inhibit us from becoming healers ourselves, a characteristic that one might expect believing people of prayer to be. Restoring this aspect of the soul has the effect of re-digging the wells from which the rivers of living water emanate from.

HEALED PEOPLE ARE FREE TO HEAL OTHERS

And as ye go, preach, saying, The kingdom of heaven is at hand. Heal the sick, cleanse the lepers, raise the dead, cast out devils: freely ye have received, freely give (Matthew 10:7-8).

Praying for healing of the innermost parts has been very effective in my ministry. My prayers have been to heal the innermost parts of the belly from damaging words, false accusations and events in life that have brought spirits of fear and immobilizing beliefs and feelings. I heal the wounds by the anointing resident within me. The feelings and physical reactions of the person are quite intense and freedom is often instantaneous. When I was first led to pray along these lines I was surprised at how effective and immediate the results were. By continuing to pray this way, I have noticed a quantum leap in deliverance and the recipients of prayer report advancement in life. It is as if chains were removed from areas within them that had held them back in life. Praise God He is teaching us to be more effective and is showing us how to liberate many who have been captive for decades.

Here are some scriptures which reveal Gods design for the inward parts which when restored to wholeness become a powerhouse of unlimited healing potential. As you are restored you will heal others.

> Who hath put wisdom in the inward parts? or who hath given understanding to the heart? (Job 38:36)

> Behold, thou desirest truth in the inward parts: and in the hidden *part* thou shalt make me to know wisdom (Psalms 51:6).

> Counsel in the heart of man *is like* deep water; but a man of understanding will draw it out (Proverbs 20:5).

A man of understanding will draw out the counsel that is reserved in an endless reservoir contained within the heart. God has put wisdom and understanding within our inward parts, but through fractures this resource more valuable than rubies has become inaccessible or hidden from our view. Heal the fracture and a release of wisdom and understanding become a purified well of salvation which many will drink from.

What is the sign that we are broken rendering wisdom and understanding inaccessible to us?

> A wholesome tongue is a tree of life: but perverseness therein is a breach in the spirit (Proverbs 15:4).

In Noah Websters' American Dictionary of the English Language 1828 Edition we find a very telling definition of the word "perverse":

Perverse: a. pervers'. [L. perversus. See pervert.]

1. Literally: turned aside; hense, distorted from the right.

2. Obstinate in the wrong; disposed to be contrary; stubborn; untractable

3. Cross; petulant; peevish; disposed to cross and vex.

When I encounter a person and listen to what they say the words are very telling. If their tongue is wholesome it is void of perverseness. But when the words are distorted from God's design and obstinately defended I realize that a breach has occurred. This person has been deeply hurt. In the inward parts, wisdom and understanding is unavailable to them. Sometimes they are not so pleasant to be around. The perverted reality of their inner world is a sign to me that the breach is a big problem in their life.

But as a servant of the Lord I can heal the breach within their Spirit, the hidden man of the heart, their innermost being, whatever term you use, they can be healed deep in their inward parts. As truth, wisdom and understanding return to them, they become functional again.

Steve was a room-mate of mine while I attended Bible College. Steve was very unusual. He did very strange things like roll on the floor for hours on end laughing uncontrollably and would sit beside you making strange facial expressions and an assortment of other things. He talked endlessly about the things that troubled him and how God was unfair and sent people to hell and that you can have no fun or you will sin and end up going to hell.

One day I asked him why he acted so strange. He told me that he was told by Dick Mills a very respected travelling prophet that he would meet a man that would help him to know how to live and since then he would act strange around people hoping that he would encounter that man who would straighten him out and help him to move forward in life. I didn't know it then but as it turns out I was the man.

Steve worked in a convenience store across the street from the dorm until midnight each night. After returning home he wanted to talk. Knowing that I had to be in class early the next morning I dreaded him coming home because I knew that I would miss my rest.

Steve couldn't help himself so he talked whether you had time for him or whether you didn't. One night, after weeks of getting very little sleep, I heard Steve coming into the parking lot in his truck, so I quickly buried my head under my pillow and pretended to be asleep. But the Lord spoke to me and told me to sit up because he wanted me to talk to Steve that night. I said OK but this better be good because you know I have missed a lot of sleep.

As soon as Steve came in he began talking but I was waiting to see what Jesus wanted to do. In a word of knowledge God showed me that Steve had a dad who was very religious, strict and ultra- demanding and was raised in an environment of law, judgment and perfectionism. As a result Steve believed that you had to be perfect or else you might go to hell. He struggled to please his dad who rarely praised Steve but instead pointed out his flaws and suggested ways he might improve. Steve who naturally had a very funny sense of humor had to hide it from his dad because his dad did not like it.

Steve saw God as he did his father unfair and stern and Satan gained an advantage over Steve by reinforcing the lie that God was unfair and unloving.

As I told Steve what the Lord was showing me he saw the lie he had believed about God and how he had been deceived. I told him that God would not show me these things if he did not want to heal Steve so I offered to pray for him. He agreed. When I prayed for him, the breach in his spirit or his inward parts were healed as God shined the light of His truth into Steve's inward parts.

Immediately Steve changed. It was as if someone flipped a switch and he was healed. He went from being very difficult to spend time with to being the guy everyone sought out to spend time with. His God-given personality was restored and his sense of humor, now welcomed in an environment of love, was the source of many wonderful hilarious memories. It was that dramatic. The change was unbelievable.

On that day the perverseness in his speech (the sign of a breach in his spirit) disappeared as a result of his inner world being healed. I tell you God got my attention that day. I know people can suddenly and undeniably be healed in a dramatic fashion.

I have to say I did not know that God could use me to minister to Steve like that, but now I know he can. I am much more useful now because I have desired to know what causes such hurt and what is the cure. Restoring the soul.

It seems that the rivers of living water contained in my belly flow out from me to heal the broken parts within others.

Healing which transcends worldly, non-biblical methods, and a transition from dependence on our understanding in favor of acknowledging God in all our ways is *God's answer to our broken windshield; the fractured soul.*

The answer is hidden in Christ, in God. In the care of God, as your soul becomes redeemed, you can rely less on your past ways of operating and are free to trust God. As you experience His faithfulness you begin to develop a track record of trusting God. As you trust Him to help you see the right ways, you are able to see Him as He is. He proves His love for you and helps you to learn and choose His ways. You come to realize that His hopes for you are good. This is how trust is built.

We cannot do this on our own. We need to be fully reliant on God. When we realize that our files are incomplete and have been corrupted, we must find out God's plan, acknowledging Him and trusting Him to direct us into freedom. This freedom in not so much about relearning the old ways as it is in learning God's ways. His files are not corrupted. They are complete, undefiled and absolutely trustworthy. It is a whole new way of thinking and being that leads to life.

It gives me hope to believe that whatever problem I face, God knows how to deliver me, guide me and open my understanding to see the situation as He does. This makes more sense than operating as I always did before. The results are far superior. When you acknowledge Him in the details, He will teach you His way and direct your steps.

As you read these words you are seeing much deeper than you have before and now realize that you may have a breach in your spirit that has held you back. It is like a ceiling that has been over your life for many years, but today in the name of Jesus God is healing you. Even now there is a release of previously inaccessible emotions. Just wipe the tears away as God continues to heal the breach. This really is the day when the deep wells of salvation, wells that you know have great power, will flow with power and bring healing to you and to others.

Words that damaged you, false accusations, gossip, slander and lying tongues which brought trouble. All these words I condemn and break their power over you so that their negative effect is nullified this day in Jesus name.

I prophesy that Jesus whose name is as an ointment poured forth is rescuing you now. By His mighty resurrection power He is pulling you out from the mouth of the lion as a beloved sheep that has wandered away into danger but is now rejoicing in the day of His visitation. He is performing a miracle in you that will release an endless flow of miracles. Your inward parts, now healed, will become a mighty stream of endless power. Your strength is returning to you today. You are vital and your serotonin levels are increasing as your body is adjusting to your healing and releasing joy unspeakable. Thank you Father for your wisdom and understanding and truth returning to the inward parts. Wisdom exceedingly much and largeness of heart becomes easily accessible from this day forward in Jesus name.

2

THE POTTER'S WHEEL

> But now, O LORD, thou art our father; we are
> the clay, and thou our potter; and we all are the
> work of thy hand (Isaiah 64:8).

Isaiah was witnessing the day when the sons of Adam would
become the sons of God. These sons would see accurately
and declare…**"now"** thou, O LORD art our father; we are the
clay, and thou art the potter; and we all are the work of thy
hand.

Jeremiah also witnessed the change of covenant. God was
taking the first creation and remaking it into another vessel or
a new creation in the last Adam, Jesus Christ.

> Then I went down to the potter's house, and,
> behold, he wrought a work on the wheels. And
> the vessel that he made of clay was marred in the
> hand of the potter: so he made it again another

vessel, as seemed good to the potter to make *it* (Jeremiah 18:3–4).

The first Adam, who was made from the clay of the earth, was marred, therefore the potter made another vessel out of the clay, which seemed good to the potter. The potter is not our old father, Adam, but our new Father who is Our Lord. In this change of parentage a terrific miracle takes place, that of adoption.

> **Adopt:** v.t. [L. *adopto*, of *ad* and *opto*, to desire or choose.]
>
> 1. To take a stranger into one's family, as a son and heir; to take one who is not a child and treat him as one, giving him a title to the privileges and rights of a child.
>
> 2. In a spiritual sense, to receive the sinful children of men into the invisible church, and into God's favor and protection, by which they become heirs of salvation by Christ.

Our Father's desire was to choose for His own, the seed of a stranger (us), to be transformed in a way pleasing to Him, to become His own children.

> He came unto his own, and his own received him not. But as many as received him, to them gave he power to become the sons of God, even to them that believe on his name (John 1:11–12).

The sons of Adam are all officially dead in Christ. The Lamb of God, Jesus, was slain for the first Adam's transgression, on the cross so that humankind would know life. In Christ's resurrection God adopts strangers (another man's children) as His own with full title to the privileges and rights of a child. When we become born again we are no longer sons of Adam, but are now the sons of God. Our full title to the privileges and rights of a child are equal to that of Christ.

Behold, what manner of love the Father hath bestowed upon us, that we should be called the sons of God: therefore the world knoweth us not, because it knew him not (1 John 3:1).

THE LION

How does a lion become a lion? A lion is a lion because he is born a lion. A lion once born a lion could never exist as anything else. Even if a lion were raised by a family of poodles this does not change it into a poodle. Its DNA makes it what it is. Even if its behavior is altered through association, genetically it remains a lion. Why? Because it was born a lion.

The Lion of the tribe of Judah is the genetic blueprint for everyone who is born again. He was the first born from the dead and is the one who brings many sons to glory.

> And I saw a strong angel proclaiming with a loud voice. Who is worthy to open the book, and to loose the seals thereof? And no man in heaven, nor in earth, neither under the earth, was able to open the book, neither to look thereon. And I wept much, because no man was found worthy to open and to read the book, neither to look thereon. And one of the elders saith unto me, Weep not: behold, the Lion of the tribe of Judah, the Root of David, hath prevailed to open the book, and to loose the seven seals thereof (Revelation 5:1–5).

When Jesus, a man born of a woman under the Law, died on the cross, He was representing the entire race of Adam. Having kept the Law as a man in perfect obedience He prevailed over death. But He was not raised from the dead as a son of Adam, but rose from the dead as the Son of God. A new creation now housed the old vessel, a new DNA in the spirit began with the power of an endless life. The day He was raised in newness of life, is that day that God the Father declared, "Thou art my Son, *this day* have I begotten thee." He was begotten out from the dead Adamic race into a new species. A new creation had been born.

> God hath fulfilled the same unto us their children, in that he hath raised up Jesus again; as it is also written in the second psalm, Thou art my Son, this day have I begotten thee (Acts 13:33).

> Giving thanks unto the Father, which hath made us meet to be partakers of the inheritance of the saints in light. Who hath delivered us from the power of darkness, and hath translated us into the kingdom of his dear Son. In whom we have redemption through his blood, even the forgiveness of sins. Who is the image of the invisible God, the firstborn of every creature (Colossians 1:11–16).

Jesus was raised from the dead, not in Adam's image but in the image of God, the firstborn Son of the new creation. As sons and daughters we are born of God in His image. We possess His DNA. The DNA of God is housed within us. The new man is the inward man, the child of God.

The prophets looked into our day and saw the regeneration. Sons of Adam die and sons of God emerge from the dead in Christ.

> And Jesus said unto them, Verily I say unto you, That ye which have followed me, in the *regeneration* when the Son of man shall sit in the throne of his glory, ye also shall sit upon twelve

thrones, judging the twelve tribes of Israel
(Matthew 19:28, italics mine).

Not by works of righteousness which we have
done, but according to his mercy he saved us, by
the washing of *regeneration*, and renewing of the
Holy Ghost (Titus 3:5, italics mine).

When you are born into the family of God, you are part
of the new creation. You don't have to try to become a new
creation; you already are one by birth. You were born that way
when you accepted Christ. Just as a lion is born a Lion, you
were born as a son of God.

Through the new birth we have become His workman-
ship in Christ Jesus, the last Adam. We have a new Father; our
Father is God, He is the potter and through the work He has
done, a new vessel was created out of the old lifeless one. When
Isaiah saw the change of covenant he likened it to the potter's
clay. The potter has turned things upside down from the way
they were.

Surely your turning of things upside down shall
be esteemed as the potter's clay: for shall the
work say of him that made it, He made me not?
or shall the thing framed say of him that framed
it, He had no understanding? (Isaiah 29:16).

Isaiah looked forward to the result of this act of God that
would turn things upside down. This work would be so amazing that men would marvel at it. Whole cultures would be
turned into the purposes of the Potter. Even a people that were
not called by His name would become the people of God.

In Thessalonica, the Book of Acts tells us that the people
protested the coming of those who have turned the world
upside down.

Now when they had passed through Amphipolis and Apollonia, they came to Thessalonica, where was a synagogue of the Jews. And Paul, as his manner was, went in unto them, and three sabbath days reasoned with them out of the scriptures. Opening and alleging, that Christ must needs have suffered, and risen again from the dead; and that this Jesus, whom I preach unto you, is Christ. And some of them believed, and consorted with Paul and Silas; and of the devout Greeks a great multitude, and of the chief women not a few. But the Jews which believed not, moved with envy, took unto them certain lewd fellows of the baser sort, and gathered a company, and set all the city on an uproar, and assaulted the house of Jason, and sought to bring them out to the people. And when they found them not, they drew Jason and certain brethren unto the rulers of the city, crying. *These that have turned the world upside down are come hither also.* Whom Jason hath received: and these all do contrary to the decrees of Caesar, saying that there is another king, *one* Jesus (Acts 17:1-7, italics mine).

Our Father the potter has turned things upside down. In so doing He has made the crooked things straight. Our God has fixed the problem. He has saved us with a master stroke of genius.

Arise, and go down to the potter's house, and there I will cause thee to hear my words (Jeremiah 18:2).

Potter, n. [from pot.] One whose occupation is to make earthen vessels.

But in a great house there are not only vessels of gold and of silver, but also of wood and of earth; and some to honour, and some to dishonour. If a man therefore purges himself from these, he shall be a vessel unto honour, sanctified, and meet for the master's use, *and* prepared unto every good work. Flee also youthful lusts: but follow righteousness, faith, charity, peace, with them that call on the Lord out of a pure heart. But foolish and unlearned questions avoid, knowing that they do gender strifes.

And the servant of the Lord must not strive; but be gentle unto all *men*, apt to teach, patient, In meekness instructing those that oppose themselves; if God peradventure will give them repentance to the acknowledging of the truth; And *that* they may recover themselves out of the snare of the devil, who are taken captive by him at his will (2 Timothy 2:20–26).

We have passed from death to life. Now our individual mission is to become a vessel unto honor, a vessel that is sanctified, qualified for the use the master has intended and prepared; ready to be employed as it seems good to the Potter. Every good work is possible by the vessel that has yielded to its predestinated purpose.

Surely your turning of things upside down shall be esteemed as the potter's clay: for shall the work say of him that made it, He made me not? or shall the thing framed say of him that framed it, He had no understanding? (Isaiah 29:16).

Understanding that we have not made ourselves is important, otherwise we will continue to live as mere men who are not regenerated. Knowing the intention of God for our lives is important. We need to know how we are designed to function as His sons to insure that we don't waste our lives.

"They have burned incense to vanity"

> Now therefore go to speak to the men of Judah, and to the inhabitants of Jerusalem, saying, Thus saith the LORD; Behold, I frame evil against you, and devise a device against you: return ye now every one from his evil way, and make your ways and your doings good. And they said, There is no hope: but we will walk after our own devices, and we will every one do the imagination of his evil heart. Therefore thus saith the LORD; Ask ye now among the heathen, who hath heard such things: the virgin of Israel hath done a very horrible thing (Jeremiah 18:11–13).

Speaking to Judah and to the inhabitants of Jerusalem the Lord begged them to turn from their evil ways and to make their ways good and their works good. Instead of returning to the Lord they continued in their ways claiming hopelessness as an excuse to not obey Him. They wanted to forget God.

> Because my people hath forgotten me, they have burned incense to vanity, and they have caused them to stumble in their ways from the ancient paths, to walk in paths, in a way not cast up (Jeremiah 18:15).

In scripture the burning of incense is usually an act of worship. When incense is burned it releases a fragrance that permeates a house with the odor. To depart from the ancient paths to worship the edifices of one's imagination is vanity. Vanity is a stench that drowns out the intended destiny of God's purposes for His people. When men walk in vanity they stumble away from God and they walk in their own ways after the imagination of their hearts. To intentionally forget God is always the precursor to degeneration and destruction.

> And even as they did not like to retain God in *their* knowledge, God gave them over to a reprobate mind, to do those things which are not convenient (Romans 1:28).

A warning from God is the greatest blessing one can receive. It means He is offering us an opportunity to return from doing those things that hinder us. These bad ways and bad works prevent us from knowing God as He really is. They leave us at the mercy of our own intellect; worshipping and burning incense to our vain patterns of repetitive foolishness.

> A fool hath no delight in understanding, but that his heart may discover itself (Proverbs 18:2).

> He that refuseth instruction despiseth his own soul: but he that heareth reproof getteth understanding (Proverbs 15:32).

God in His mercy, through wisdom and understanding, saves us from our own ways. He has a new plan for His sons and daughters. When we delight in understanding, receiving instruction and taking heed when we are reproved, we are restored to health and a life of wholeness.

> Doth not wisdom cry? and understanding put forth her voice? (Proverbs 8:1).

He is always wooing us to enter into the safety and blessings of relationship with Himself. Turning from dead works and of faith towards God is the way.

The following two verses in the Bible define **understanding.**

> The fear of the LORD is the beginning of wisdom: and the knowledge of the holy is understanding (Proverbs 9:10).

> And unto man he said, Behold, the fear of the Lord, that is wisdom; and to depart from evil is understanding (Job 28:28).

To forsake evil and pursue of the knowledge of the holy is the way of *understanding*. Those of an understanding heart will forsake evil and pursue the knowledge of the holy. This seems to be a central theme of the book of Proverbs. The foundations of wisdom and understanding are essential to living a godly life and being blessed.

Below are a sampling of this theme and ways that destruction follows those who lack understanding and how blessing follows those who seek understanding.

> Understanding is a wellspring of life unto him that hath it: but the instruction of fools is folly (Proverbs 16:22).

> A wise man will hear, and will increase learning; and a man of understanding shall attain unto wise counsels (Proverbs 1:5).

> Forsake the foolish, and live; and go in the way of understanding (Proverbs 9:6).

In the lips of him that hath understanding wisdom is found: but a rod *is* for the back of him that is void of understanding (Proverbs 10:13).

> **❝** *When God is not intimately known, He cannot be accurately shown.*
>
> - **Robert Madu**

Folly is joy to him that is destitute of wisdom: but a man of understanding walketh uprightly (Proverbs 15:21).

The prince that wanteth understanding *is* also a great oppressor: *but* he that hateth covetousness shall prolong *his* days (Proverbs 28:16).

A lack of understanding *in the prince* causes him to oppress people. It is incredible to think about the consequences of national suffering when a nation's rulers do not seek after understanding.

And we know that all things work together for good to them that love God, to them who are the called *according to his purpose*. For whom he did foreknow, he also did predestinate *to be* conformed to the image of his Son, that he might be the firstborn among many brethren. Moreover whom he did predestinate, them he also called: and whom he called, them he also justified: and whom he justified, them he also glorified (Romans 8:28–30, italics mine).

The Potter's work does not end when we are born again. Something extraordinary begins to unfold. The purpose predestined by the Potter, imagined long ago, and purposed in Himself was to conform us into the image of His Son.

Having made known unto us the mystery of his will, according to his good pleasure which he hath *purposed in himself*, That in the dispensation of the fullness of times he might gather together in one all things in Christ, both which are in heaven, and which are on earth; *even* in him (Ephesians 1:9–10, italics mine).

If we are to know God's purpose for our lives we must come under the lordship of the King. When we do this He puts us under the authority of the Holy Spirit. This authority encompasses every mandate from God, given to the Holy Spirit, for every son and daughter that He has adopted.

3

THE INWARD MAN

The spirit of man is the candle of the lord; searching all the inward parts of the belly (Proverbs 20:27).

For which cause we faint not; but though our outward man perish, yet the inward man is renewed day by day (2 Corinthians 4:16).

From the mid 1970's up to 1988 I was steeped in sin and bound with addictions. Drugs and alcohol were an everyday part of my life. An acquaintance of mine, Betty Cherry and I worked together at the same real estate company in Gatlinburg, Tennessee from 1983–1985. We were very much in the party scene as were most of the other people with whom we worked.

For whatever reasons we went to work for different companies, but found ourselves working at the same company again in 1987. I was the same person, but Betty had changed. Later she shared with me that when we worked together before, she had been a back-slidden Christian, running from God and was living the same life of sin that I had been. She told me that things had changed and she had surrendered to God and was living her life as it was meant to be lived, free from sin. She really had changed and would not do the things she used to but instead devoted her time to going to church and living in the presence of God.

One day while I was in a very low point of my life I confided in Betty about my problem with drugs and alcohol and the misery that my lifestyle had brought. I asked her to pray for me. She agreed and I went back to work. Later that day she asked me if I would go to church with her that night. I thought I had nothing to lose; and even though a part of me resisted the idea, I agreed.

A revival meeting was taking place at a little country church pastored by Brother Glen Parton, who I later learned was Dolly Parton's uncle. The visiting evangelist preached a passionate message, most of which I have forgotten, because I was so caught up with the inner turmoil raging inside me at the time.

I remember an invitation at the end of his message encouraging anyone who needed Jesus to set them free. I was in my seat wrestling with whether or not to come to God with my impossible hopelessness. After a few others had gone forward for prayer, I went up. When he prayer for me he laid his hand upon me and prayed in other tongues. As I waited, hoping for the help he had promised, I remember thinking, *God I know you can help me if you will.* The moment this thought went through my mind a gentle wisp of air seemed to blow right through my head.

Instantly, as the air passed through me something left me and great joy flooded my soul. When the evangelist stopped praying he looked at me. I declared, "It's gone!" He shouted "praise God brother" and gave me a big hug. At that point I felt as if my innocence had been restored. Standing there at 29 years of age, for the first time since being a young child, I felt clean. I had been set free by the hand of God through Jesus Christ His Son.

Betty asked me back to church the next day, this time I did not hesitate and returned with her every night for the next month or so. Right after my conversion, she asked me if I had received the Holy Ghost. I asked her what she meant. She fished through her purse and produced a mini book entitled *Why Tongues?* by Kenneth E. Hagin. She said I was to read the book and to look up the scriptures used in the booklet and report back to her in a couple of days.

I knew Betty was pretty wild back in the days we partied together, but I was not prepared for how aggressively bold she was while under the influence of the Holy Ghost. I was about to find out.

She asked if I had read the book. I said that I had. She asked if I wanted to be baptized in the Holy Ghost, I said that I did, so she leaped forward placed her hand on my head and commanded me to receive the Holy Ghost.

Next thing I knew I was on the floor and this wild woman was on top of me with her lips an inch from my ear saying, "I command you to speak in tongues." So I just opened my mouth and did what she said. I began speaking in other tongues right there on the floor of Glen Parton's church.

Having understood that there was a war raging for my soul, and, that by becoming a part of God's family I had escaped the kingdom of darkness through believing in Jesus Christ, I knew that this war was serious and that in order to stay safe I must become fully established in the Word of God. I also understood that I needed to obey the instructions that are laid out in God's Word and to receive instruction from His servants that He had placed in my life.

I looked to Betty for help and guidance. She was very loving and kind and had my best interests at heart. At times she shocked me, but I knew that she loved me I trusted her and accepted her as she was. It reminds me of a relationship with a mother. They are not perfect nor are the relationships always pleasant but the binding of the heart connection and the history that you have is one of love.

Betty also granted me the greatest honor ever bestowed upon me. This honor would be the single most important key to victory I would ever discover.

She sat me down and began to teach me about the importance of remaining in continual prayer. This lesson was to be about a particular type of prayer that would turn my life upside down and drew me increasingly into the supernatural kingdom of God where miracles are the rule, not the exception.

It was the type of prayer that revealed to me that God had a purpose for every person within His kingdom that cannot be understood by simply going to church and reading the Bible, but must be spiritually understood.

The understanding had to come from the part of me that was recreated in the image of Christ Jesus, the inward man. The inward man is otherwise known as the new man, the hidden man of the heart, the new creation.

I learned through Betty that this inward man had the ability to touch the supernatural world, in a similar way that my mind is able to touch the intellectual world, or that my body is able to touch the physical world through its five physical senses. This inward man has been raised with Christ and made to sit with Him in heavenly places.

The natural mind cannot understand it nor does the physical body have the ability to touch this supernatural world by access through the five physical senses. The supernatural realm is the domain of the inner man who, like God, is a spirit and therefore has gained the privilege and access through sonship into the spiritual realm and kingdom.

In the same way that I become a citizen of the earth, by being born into it, I also become a citizen of the kingdom of God through the birth of the new man. As a person living on the earth I have rights and responsibilities, privileges and areas of authority. I learn what safety is, why it is important, and through trial and error, I learn how to live the best life possible. This best life possible is then taught to the next generation as we rise to the responsibility to teach our children how to conduct themselves and how to live meaningful and productive lives.

Similarly in the kingdom of God we have been given stature, authority, righteousness, wisdom, sanctification, redemption and all things that pertain to life and godliness through Christ Jesus. It is this inner man who through the new birth has been baptized into Christ Jesus. This new man did not earn it, nevertheless it is as much his as a baby's toe is a part of his body. The kingdom and everything in the kingdom have become his birthright through his inheritance as a joint heir with Jesus Christ. Inheritance is received through succession, and for no other reason. It is not earned but passed down from the testator Jesus Christ.

The day I received the baptism in the Holy Ghost, was the day I received the key that unlocked my understanding of the supernatural realm and made available to me the entire kingdom of God. I received the supernatural language of praying in other tongues. This language is the language of the spirit realm, the language of the supernatural world, the language given to the inner man. This is a language that God has chosen as a direct link between the spirit of man and the spirit of God; a Spirit to spirit language of communication, hitherto unknown to me and available only to the inner man.

Betty challenged me to pray in tongues daily and for long periods of time. By doing so, I worked directly with God, through the inner man, to work out those things in my life that cause me to fail and establish me as a member of His family. As a parent teaches a child and prepares them for life in this world, God has a plan to do the same for every child born into His spiritual family. Praying from the inner man, in other tongues, would insure that the process of maturity and becoming functional within His plan for me would be a success. It would qualify and activate within me, the gifts of the Holy Ghost and the callings of God.

Betty warned me that Satan is terrified that I will operate from the inner man by praying in unknown tongues. She said that Satan will try anything he can to discourage me from praying this way. His methods of trying to stop me would vary. He would tell me that it was a waste of time. He would suggest that since my mind did not know what I was saying, how did I know that I was not cursing God or mocking him? He would tell me that I had been made into a fool for participating in such nonsense.

Her advice to me was that anytime I had such thoughts that I was to tell Satan to shut up and to pray all the more. So I followed her advice, which wasn't easy. He did exactly what she warned me about. In addition, circumstances and day-to-day distractions had to be secondary because I was determined to pray in other tongues and live in the supernatural realm of which I had become a part.

I was determined to make praying in tongues part of my everyday life. I vowed not to allow Satan to talk me out of it. In spite of the many trials from the flesh, and the opinions of others, I remained persistent in my efforts of building continuous prayer into my daily routines.

Betty taught me that when I did not know how to pray that the Spirit of God would help my infirmities, making intercession for me through my praying in other tongues. She said that the Spirit of God knows what the will of God is for my future and would pray me right through any unknown needs or problems to fulfill His plan. It is when you allow the Holy Spirit to activate God's plan that you qualify for all things working together for good to those who love God and are called according to his purposes (Romans 8:28). It is then that you have submitted to the predestination of being conformed to the image of His dear Son. You must yield to the hands of the Potter, and through this process, allow Him to perfect His plan for your life from within. The Spirit of God knows the personal plan for your life, but He also knows how you fit into the overall plan for the entire body of Christ. So as you pray in the Spirit you grant God access to perfect His plans concerning you.

I reasoned that I didn't know how to pray anyway, so why not get the Spirit of God involved with my spirit in order to bring His plan to pass in my life. So I prayed in tongues when I woke up, on the way to work, during breaks in the day, and on the way to church, all through the church service and on the way home. This went on for months. There were times of great joy, times of doubt and confusion, battles between my spirit and my flesh (the new ways of seeing and thinking were doing battle with the old ways). A war was being waged in the realm of the spirit but Betty assured me I would be victorious if I held my ground and continued to activate this supernatural prayer language.

When you have chosen a path, it seems easier to walk if you have relationship with others who have made the same commitment. I began to look for others who spoke in other tongues. I was looking for pastors, evangelists, teachers who not only taught about praying in tongues and walking in the spirit, but who do so continually.

I began to notice that these people talked and behaved differently. They seemed to really know God. They were having supernatural experiences that defied human reasoning and brought tangible evidence of the supernatural kingdom in which they lived. They were healing the sick, casting out devils, preaching and teaching the Bible with obvious authority and powerful results. This kingdom that I had discovered through praying in tongues was a kingdom where anything is possible to those who believed.

Other Christians I knew were shocked at the degree of revelation knowledge I had as I excitedly preached and taught them what the Holy Spirit was giving me through this language. They could not believe that I had only been walking with God a few short months. I kept hearing them say they thought I had been a Christian for a long time. To be honest, having nothing to compare myself too, I thought that my experience was normal. I thought the relationship I had with God was what everyone experienced . . . I was wrong.

Betty had introduced me to the road less travelled. It was not a road trampled down by the masses of Christianity, but one that only a remnant travelled. My inward man was creating an internal environment of sustainable breakthrough. This breakthrough found its source in the true vine, a method of abiding that sadly, many do not know about. I experienced a free flow of the power on the inside to take the kingdom by force.

> Verily I say unto you, Among them that are born of women there hath not risen a greater than John the Baptist: notwithstanding he that is least in the kingdom of heaven is greater than he. And from the days of John the Baptist until now the kingdom of heaven suffereth violence, and the violent take it by force (Matthew 11:11–12).

The kingdom of God came with a promise that would turn the world upside down. Jesus declared that there has never been a man born of a woman greater than John the Baptist, but here Jesus is offering us an x-ray of the new creature, the hidden man of the heart, the spirit man who would be born from above in the new creation. Every man born in the new birth would begin his walk with God as one greater than John the Baptist, the greatest of all Old Testament saints. The New Testament saint would be capable of doing the works of Jesus and greater. You can probably see the wheels turning in the heads of the disciples as Jesus made these bold and revealing statements concerning the new creation.

This kingdom would prove to be the biggest threat to the status quo ever revealed and would most certainly turn the world upside down, revealing the glory of God and the wisdom of God like never before in all of history. What a kingdom. This is a kingdom against which the gates of hell are blocking and resisting your entrance with great force and intent. A kingdom that only the aggressive and those willing to take up arms, are able to claim as their own. This is the kingdom of God within you.

Having entered, I found it unusual that so few people had found it. That is the truth. As in the prayer "thy kingdom come" His kingdom had come to me. I was swimming in it. It was full of righteousness, peace and joy in the Holy Ghost. It is amazing to me that so many are hoping for the kingdom of God to come to them, not realizing that they already possess the kingdom of God within themselves.

> And when he was demanded of the Pharisees, when the kingdom of God should come, he answered them and said, The kingdom of God cometh not with observation: Neither shall they say, Lo here! or, lo there! for, behold, the kingdom of God is within you (Luke 17:20–21).

The hurdle for most people is that they have not understood how to access the kingdom within them. The inward man is the one who has access. The new creation within is the one who is designed to rule and reign with Christ. Unfortunately he keeps getting passed over for promotion by the old man who sabotages the purposes of God by maintaining control of our lives. This is the greatest challenge to your calling and election that you will face. Your inward man must take his rightful place.

I have seen servants upon horses, and princes
walking as servants upon the earth (Ecclesiastes
10:7).

In Ecclesiastes Solomon is perplexed by this observation.
**He has seen servants upon horses and princes walking
as servants upon the earth.** In Solomon's observation the servant, who was holding the reins, was the one giving the orders
to the prince who was operating as a slave.

In the new creation, the old man has been declared dead.
We are commanded to reckon him dead by faith, putting him
off and putting on the new man that is created in righteousness
and true holiness. The inward man is the prince. Then why is
it that the old man is still in the saddle while the inward man
(who has been declared to be greater than John the Baptist) has
been reduced to the role of a slave, even though he is a king?
He is being forced to serve the old man when in fact he has the
title and authority to reign.

This is the case if we are not subservient to the Potter's will.
He is the one who is raising a king who has been endowed with
great wealth, right in the middle of an earthen vessel. *Mastering
the earthen vessel by the rule of the inner man is the plan of the
Potter.* To this end He has placed the kingdom in the inner man
and sent the Holy Ghost to mentor the king within in all things
concerning the kingdom.

This can only be achieved by the leadership of the inward
man with the guidance of the Holy Ghost. When the old man
is calling the shots, the work of the Potter is delayed until such
time as the divine order is restored.

Over the years I have occasionally lost my way during times
of tribulation. Even though I knew I had found something that
works, I quit doing it. Instead of the new man calling the shots
the old man was forcing his will. I learned that times of fasting
were required to deliver me from unbelief when the old man
wouldn't get out of the saddle. I discovered that fasting is the

meat tenderizer of the flesh. In combination with praying in the Holy Ghost, fasting can defeat whatever resistance the flesh might muster up.

> *Praying in the Holy Ghost restores divine order*
> *by knocking the old man off the horse*
> *and restoring the prince to his rightful place in the saddle.*

Saul of Tarsus was knocked of his horse. When he finally jumped back in the saddle he did so as Paul the Apostle to the Gentiles. He climbed back up, not as the old man, but through the grace of God, climbed onto the saddle as a new creature, full of the Holy Ghost, who later declared to the Corinthians:

I thank my God, I speak with tongues more than ye all (1 Corinthians. 14:18).

Prayerlessness seems always to be the thing that causes us to run aground. I now understand why Betty so adamantly insisted that this was the single most important key she could give me. Betty and I lost touch over the years, but her love for me and devotion to God pointed the way during a critical juncture in my life.

Jesus blessed me with a Betty Cherry when I needed her most. I pray that God will bless you with your own Betty Cherry who will give you the truth, and give it to you straight.

But we have this treasure in earthen vessels, that the excellency of the power may be of God, and not of us (2 Corinthians 4:7).

A seasoned believer understands what keys of victory can lead you into contending **for the faith that was once delivered unto the saints**. If they know what they are doing they will deliver you into the hands of the Potter and cause you to become dependent on the Holy Ghost and His workings within your new nature. The excellency of the power is of God and not of us, yet that power is resident within the inward man.

The inward man is the new creation; everything concerning the kingdom of heaven comes through the inward man. He is the gateway between heaven and earth.

4

THE SPIRIT OF WISDOM AND UNDERSTANDING

Before the law came through Moses the children of Israel were slaves in the Land of Egypt. They had no rights, but were the property of the Pharaoh; prior to that they were free. There was no Law. They had a covenant with God through Abraham, Isaac and Jacob and were God's people under that covenant.

Before the law came God dealt with His people through covenant. The idea of covenant goes way back. A covenant is an agreement between two parties. In ancient times, a people small in number, would go to another tribe or peoples and make a covenant. The covenant was a promise between the two peoples. The terms of the covenant would be negotiated, which would include blessings and curses. Curses for the party that broke the covenant were very severe. The blessings were the rewards or benefits enjoyed between the two parties when the covenant was upheld. Usually the covenant would include protection from peoples outside the covenant and the sharing of resources between the peoples within covenant.

Abraham came into covenant with God. He was to circumcise all the male children as a sign of the covenant. *The difference in this covenant was that it came without any curses attached to it, only blessings.* As another man's sons (Adam) they were not Gods sons. They were not adopted into God's family until Christ. Under the covenant God made with Abraham, Abraham simply had to believe that God was able to do what He said. He entered into the covenant by faith. Faith in God meant keeping His word and nothing else.

When the law that God put in place through Moses came, the terms of the covenant changed. Like covenants that were made between men, God's covenant with man included blessings as well as curses. If you kept the Law there was blessing associated in doing so. If you forsook the Law there were curses associated in doing so. Much like a contract with an employer, if you show up for work and do what is required you get a paycheck (blessing), if you fail to come in for work, would you still expect to be paid? No. Only when you meet the terms of your employment do you expect to enjoy the paycheck. Failing to keep the terms of the contract means that you will be out of favor with the boss and rejected/fired from your employment for not keeping the terms (curse). This is what it was like to be under the Law of Moses.

Under the new covenant ratified by the blood of Jesus Christ the testator, whosoever believes from his heart that God raised Jesus from the dead, and confesses Him as Lord, will be saved. He is saved through the washing of regeneration and renewing of the Holy Ghost (Titus 3:5). Man receives a new spirit as a result of the new birth. The Bible calls this new spirit the Spirit of Christ.

> But ye are not in the flesh, but in the Spirit, if
> so be that the Spirit of God dwell in you. Now
> if any man have not the Spirit of Christ, he is
> none of his. And if Christ be in you, the body is

> dead because of sin; but the Spirit is life because of righteousness. But if the Spirit of him that raised up Jesus from the dead dwell in you, he that raised up Christ from the dead shall also quicken your mortal bodies by his Spirit that dwelleth in you (Romans 8:9–11, italics mine).

Those that have believed have received the Spirit of Christ. They are born again and have received a new Spirit. The relationship changes at this point, sons of Adam are now regenerated into sons of God. Our bodies have been declared dead because of sin, but the Spirit is life because of righteousness. We are no longer under the Law and have now become heirs of God and joint heirs with Christ; we no longer operate under contract or law, but under grace.

Grace is the power of Christ by the Spirit of Christ within us enabling us to receive our full inheritance as the saints in the light and empowers us to be ministers of the kingdom. It is the birthright of sons. Sons do not earn what they have inherited; they need only claim it and put it to work for them.

> Giving thanks unto the Father, which hath made us meet to be partakers of the inheritance of the saints in light: Who hath delivered us from the power of darkness, and hath translated *us* into the kingdom of his dear Son: In whom we have redemption through his blood, *even* the forgiveness of sins: Who is the image of the invisible God, *the firstborn of every creature* (Colossians 1:11–15, italics mine).

Jesus was not the first born of every man…that was Adam, but it says he is the firstborn of every creature (the new creation).

Through the new birth we are automatically qualified to be partakers of the inheritance of the saints in light. He qualified us because we ceased being another man's sons (Adam) through death, and were raised with Christ, with a new spirit, having become the sons of God.

> For the *law of the Spirit of life in Christ Jesus hath made me free from the law of sin and death.* For what the law could not do, in that it was weak through the flesh, God sending his own Son in the likeness of sinful flesh, and for sin, condemned sin in the flesh: That the righteousness of the law might be fulfilled in us, who walk not after the flesh, but after the Spirit (Romans 8:1–4, italics mine).

A new law took over; the law of the Spirit of Life in Christ Jesus. Being in Christ, having the Spirit of Christ within us, translated us from death into life, from the kingdom of darkness into the kingdom of His dear Son through the Spirit of His Son. We are no longer slaves sold under sin, but are sons of God and heirs.

> For ye have not received the spirit of bondage again to fear; but ye have received the Spirit of adoption, whereby we cry, Abba, Father (Romans 8:15).

We have no fear of the curses of a broken contract (death) but we have been redeemed and brought into the family of God.

> For God hath not given us the spirit of fear; but of power, and of love, and of a sound mind (2 Timothy 1:7).

We already died with Christ as sons of Adam but were also raised with Christ in newness of life as the sons of God. As sons, the inheritance is guaranteed through Christ, who, under the Law, earned every blessing available under the law, by perfect obedience to the Law. This brought an inheritance to everyone born from the dead, of which He was the first.

> Being made so much better than the angels, as he hath *by inheritance* obtained a more excellent name than they (Hebrews 1:4, italics mine).

> And being found in fashion as a man, he humbled himself, and became obedient unto death, even the death of the cross. Wherefore God also hath highly exalted him, and given him a name which is above every name: That at the name of Jesus every knee should bow, of things in heaven, and things in earth, and things under the earth; And that every tongue should confess that Jesus Christ is Lord, to the glory of God the Father (Philippians 2:8–11).

This name, Jesus, is above all names and carries all authority in heaven and in earth. We have been given this Name. We have been called by this Name and we have become sons of God through this Name. The revelation of our inheritance and everything that comes with it comes to us by the Spirit.

The spirit of wisdom and revelation in the knowledge of Christ has been imparted to us. By this spirit, we explore what we have received through inheritance. Now, as sons, we explore the scriptures with the assistance of the Spirit who wrote them and receive revelation directly from God, ***needing no intermediary***.

> That the God of our Lord Jesus Christ, the Father of glory, may give unto you the spirit

of wisdom and revelation in the knowledge of him: The eyes of your understanding being enlightened; that ye may know what is the hope of his calling, and what the riches of the glory of his inheritance in the saints, And what is the exceeding greatness of his power to us-ward who believe, according to the working of his mighty power, Which he wrought in Christ, when he raised him from the dead, and set him at his own right hand in the heavenly places, Far above all principality, and power, and might, and dominion, and every name that is named, not only in this world, but also in that which is to come: And hath put all things under his feet, and gave him to be the head over all things to the church, Which is his body, the fulness of him that filleth all in all (Ephesians 1:17–23).

Paul is praying this for the church at Ephesus and to the faithful in Jesus Christ.

Paul, an apostle of Jesus Christ by the will of God, to the saints which are at Ephesus, *and to the faithful in Christ Jesus* (Ephesians 1:1, italics mine).

Not only was this prayer for them, *but it is also for everyone who is faithful in Christ Jesus.* Are you *faithful in Christ Jesus*? If so, the Spirit of wisdom and revelation in the knowledge of Him is for you.

Spiritual things are understood by spiritual beings. As a new man you are a spiritual man. He is saying that through the spirit of wisdom and revelation in the knowledge of Him, the eyes of your understanding would be enlightened, enabling you know the hope of your calling and the riches of the glory in his inheritance in the saints.

You will become familiar with the exceeding greatness of His power, toward you because you believe, the same power that raised Christ from the dead, and set Him at His own right hand above all principalities and powers and might and dominion and every name that is named not only in this world but also in the world to come and has put all things under His feet and has given Him to be the head over all things concerning the church, which is His body; the fullness of Him that filleth all in all (see Ephesians. 1:16–23).

Under the old covenant the principles of gaining wisdom and understanding were available by departing from evil and by putting into practice the Law of God.

Under the new covenant, the spirit of wisdom and revelation in the knowledge of Him brings you into intimate knowledge of your son-ship. You will be equipped for your individual calling and all the power and authority you will ever need to satisfy the requirements of your role. All of this can be known and will be revealed to you by His Spirit. The only requirement on your part is that you become an explorer. Exploring the mysteries of your inheritance and the power vested in you, is your part. Included in this exploration is activating these mysteries by taking part in the work of God. You are family now. The family has an eternal purpose and a temporal mission of which you are a part. It will require putting to work what you have been given in Christ. Those who are putting to work what they have been given are those who Paul refers to as **"the faithful in Christ Jesus."** The spirit of wisdom and revelation in the knowledge of Him will bring you into an operational understanding and activation of your service to Christ Jesus who is the head of the church.

I hope this is great news to you as it was to me. For me the best part of this good news was that I didn't need to earn any of my inheritance. The inheritance comes exclusively by birthright, an act of God's grace as He adopts us into His family when He birthed us by His Spirit into His kingdom. Praise the

Lord! This miracle of the new birth made me a son under the grace of God and delivered me from the curses of the Law. \o/ Praise God!

5

THE MAIL ROOM

When starting a new job there is an orientation period. The job of working in the mail room is the proverbial entry level position. Every person in the company has a position. Some are in command positions, other administrative positions and operational positions. **Competency** at every position is needed for the company to function at its best.

> Now there are *diversities of gifts*, but the same Spirit. And there are *differences of administrations*, but the same Lord. And there are *diversities of operations*, but it is the same God which worketh all in all. But the manifestation of the Spirit is given to every man to profit withal (1 Corinthians 12:4–7, italics mine).

In God's organization there is great wisdom. We are amply supplied with the *gifts* we need to become competent in our roles, to *administrate* our duties as we become *operational* within our family structure. But instead of being an employee, we are sons involved in the family business.

Our day of appointment is when we believe in Christ and are born again. We come into the family of God and through the operation of the Spirit of God we begin our orientation. We receive an entry level gifting when we are baptized in the Holy Ghost which causes us to be one with God, one with each other, and one with the purposes of the family business.

This *gift* is the gift of the Holy Ghost. When He comes into a son He brings with Him everything needed for you to fulfill the plan of God, both for your individual life and for your mission within the family. He knows exactly where you fit and what your roles will be.

Our family is a revelatory family. Revelation is the form of communication in the family of God and the entry level gifting is diversities of tongues. **The gift of diversities of tongues is a revelation gift**. This is the foundational gifting because revelation is the language of communication in the family business. Without the ability to receive revelation according to the family design, we will feel disconnected and dysfunctional.

Unlike earthly kingdoms where communications have to be passed from one department to the other, our God is able to communicate with every single member of His family directly and simultaneously. His communications are done through the very same Spirit that we have been given, the Holy Spirit.

HEARING FROM GOD IS THE ENTRY LEVEL COMPETENCY

Competent: a. Suitable; fit; convenient; hence sufficient, that is, fit for the purpose; adequate.

1. Suitable; adequately prepared for a purpose

2. Incident; belonging; having adequate power or right

3. Qualified; fit; having legal capacity or power

The primary goal of your orientation is to become competent in the entry level gifting of diversities of tongues. In the initial stages, praying in other tongues activates the work of the Holy Spirit in building within your spirit the **core competencies** of:

1. Hearing God.

2. Receiving revelation.

3. Obeying commands.

These core competencies will be relied upon in producing fruit _**at every level**_ of advancement. Advancement comes when your competency is tested and proven at the level you are at. Advancement is not automatic. You don't advance if you do not put to use the gifts you have been given to build the competencies required for advancement.

HOW ARE CORE COMPETENCIES ESTABLISHED?

In the movie "The Karate Kid" Daniel, played by Ralph Machio, was the son of a single mom. Mother and son had moved to a new place and the adjustment for Daniel was complicated due to a group of bullies who were part of a Karate club. Not only were they aggressive and brutal bullies, but also disciplined in martial arts. Daniel got beat up a few times, but then was rescued by Miyagi, played by Pat Morita, who played an old Japanese man who knew Karate.

Daniel wished to learn how to survive and defend himself against these young men, and wanted Miyagi to teach him Karate. Hesitantly, an old and wizened Miyagi took Daniel under his wing and trained him.

His rules were simple. Complete obedience to whatever the master wanted him to do. So the training began.

The young pupil showed up at Miyagi's house where he was put to work waxing the old man's car. This seemed odd to

Daniel because he had come to learn Karate, not to wax an old man's car. When he complained Miyagi reminded him that the lessons depended upon Daniel's complete compliance. So he decided to obey his master.

Miyagi taught Daniel the proper motions of putting the wax on the car. This was referred to as "wax on" which involved moving in a circular motion in a clockwise movement. After the wax was applied he showed him the circular counter-clockwise motion called "wax off." Anytime the instructions were not followed, Miyagi stopped Daniel and took him back to the wax on/wax off fundamentals until he performed the task correctly. In Daniel's mind, when he finished waxing the car, the Karate lessons would begin, but instead Miyagi had another car for him to wax, and another; after a couple of days the cars were all waxed and Daniel was exhausted.

Next Daniel was taught how to sand the deck. Miyagi gave Daniel a sanding block and taught him the motions of sanding the deck. When he did it wrong Miyagi would stop him, re-instruct him on the fundamental movements of sanding the deck, then Daniel would go back to work. After this he had him paint the fence.

The same instruction and correction took place. Daniel was becoming very frustrated. He got angry and complained to Miyagi that he was being taken advantage of. He accused Miyagi of using him to do all of the chores and not teaching him Karate.

Miyagi then asked Daniel to defend himself and instructed Daniel by using the same movements he had learned in waxing the cars. **"Wax on"** he commanded and took a punch at Daniel. By using this simple movement that he had learned when waxing the car, Daniel discovered that he was able to block the punch. He then gave him other commands like "sand the deck" and "paint the fence." Again he discovered that when attacked he was able to defend himself.

Daniel was waking up to the revelation that **simple movements performed in chores were the elementary movements** in the art of Karate. He already had learned the basics. They were the foundation of Karate. The beauty of it was that he had become quite competent in Karate even before he knew he had.

He got excited when he realized that he had already mastered the basics without even knowing what the master was doing. His training then advanced beyond his wildest imagination because his mind and body had already been trained, through many hours of doing the exact same movements, over and over again.

This is how competence is formed. It becomes automatic. Anything that you do over and over again becomes automatic. Receiving revelation, obeying God, performing miracles, healing the sick, casting out devils and preaching the gospel. It all becomes automatic, if you will apply yourself in obedience to the Holy Spirit. He will work within you **the daily routines** needed to build your competency in the fundamentals. When the fundamentals become routine the Holy Spirit will build upon them.

Our master in our development is the Holy Spirit. His plan is to use fundamental building blocks to qualify and prepare you through core competencies so that you can become thoroughly equipped for every good work.

The gift of diversities of tongues is the wax on/wax off of the new creation. By repetitively praying in other tongues, for hours and hours every day, you become trained in the basic entry-level dynamics of the kingdom of God; the first of which is hearing His voice.

When these habits become automatic you will master the core competency of hearing from God.

So many people are not functional because they do not understand the entry-level competencies of this new family of which we are a part. Fail to put in the daily work and you fail to become functional. But if you put in the work God will advance you according to your competence.

Since there are different kinds of tongues (diversities of tongues) other core competencies are added as you continue your training. Revelation of other kinds of tongues is built upon the core competency, like tongues for personal edification (sand the deck). **He that speaketh in an *unknown* tongue edifieth himself; but he that prophesieth edifieth the church (1 Corinthians 14:4).**

Tongues for **speaking mysteries** (paint the fence). **For he that speaketh in an *unknown* tongue speaketh not unto men, but unto God: for no man understandeth *him;* howbeit in the spirit he *speaketh mysteries* (1 Corinthians 14:2, italics mine).**

As you are beginning to see there are a variety or diversity of tongues. Tongues have different functions in personal development and as a ministry gift. *When you understand the variety of uses found in the different kinds of tongues, your revelation will take you past the confusion and unbelief that keep others from advancing.*

An example of this confusion is the misinterpretation of 1 Corinthians. 12:29–30:

> Are all apostles? are all prophets? are all teachers? are all workers of miracles? Have all the gifts of healing? do all speak with tongues? do all interpret?

Here Paul asks a question concerning **ministry gifts.** All of these questions are exclusively speaking about operations **for use when ministering to others.** An apostle is a gift to the church to build the foundations of her faith. The prophet, the teacher, the miracle workers and those who utilize the gifts of healings are also gifts that God gives to the church to edify and equip her for ministry. Tongues which are publically spoken are given by a person endowed with **this type** of tongue to *minister* as a revelation gift. This is usually followed by another person who has the **ministry gifting** of interpretation of tongues. Again these are specific **ministry gifts** used to **minister to others**. Other types of tongues are used for **personal development**.

Much confusion and division has existed within the Church because of a lack of understanding of the difference between the **ministry uses** of tongues and the different tongues **used for personal development**. *Many have thrown out the entire category as unessential because they mistakenly believe it is not for everyone.*

Imagine a corporation getting rid of the mail room and mail altogether because not everyone in the corporation has a management function. The resulting **lack of communication would cause operational paralysis.**

This is unfortunate and has kept many from being fully integrated within the family business of God. The entry level appointment is forfeited; operational dysfunction is the default due to rejecting your kingdom blueprint.

Remember it is a spiritual kingdom; a spiritual family. This kingdom has power and not everyone knows about the power. This kingdom is not of this world. Spirit beings make up this kingdom and spirit beings must operate according to its design. A new creature is a spirit being. We exist on this planet but our home is in a spiritual place, heaven. It behooves us to learn the language.

Isaiah spoke of the transition from human beings to spirit beings in regards to a new way of learning and a new method of communication that God would use to speak to us. He also predicted that many would miss this new spiritual method of communication. Isaiah said that failure to make this transition would bring them back under bondage, causing them to forfeit *rest and refreshing*. Imagine totally missing the *rest* and *refreshing* of this entry-level competency. Many have missed it. Whole denominations have forbidden it and taught against it.

Whom shall he teach knowledge? and whom shall he make to understand doctrine? them that are weaned from the milk, and drawn from the breasts. For precept must be upon precept,

precept upon precept; line upon line, line upon line; here a little, and there a little: For with stammering lips and another
tongue will he speak to this people. To whom he said, This is
the rest wherewith ye may cause the weary to rest; and this is
the refreshing: yet they would not hear (Isaiah 28:9 -12).

Paul makes reference to this prophecy when teaching on
tongues in his first letter to the Corinthians.

> Brethren, be not children in *understanding*:
> howbeit in malice be ye children, but in *under-
> standing be men*. In the law it is written, With *men
> of* other tongues and other lips will I speak unto
> this people; and yet for all that *will they not hear
> me*, saith the Lord (1 Corinthians 14:20–21,
> italics mine).

Isaiah begins with the question:

> **Whom shall he teach knowledge? and whom
> shall he make to *understand doctrine? them
> that are* weaned from the milk, *and* drawn
> from the breasts (Isaiah 28:9, italics mine).**

Paul is also exhorting the Church by saying:

> Brethren, be not children in *understanding*:
> howbeit in malice be ye children, but in *under-
> standing be men* (1 Corinthians 14:20, italics
> mine).

*Notice the connection between immaturity and those who
would not hear.*

Centuries before the Holy Spirit manifested in the speaking
of tongues God saw that some people would reject tongues.
They would miss the transition into the new method of God
speaking to and teaching His people under a new covenant.

They would indeed be born again, but they would fail to receive the supernatural language of spiritual communication. This is similar to a person who moves to a different nation with a different language, but who won't learn the language. He will forfeit the benefit of interaction with these people simply because his ability to communicate will be very limited.

Being weaned from the milk and drawn from the breast positions you for **HIM TO TEACH you knowledge** and for **YOU TO UNDERSTAND doctrine**. If you don't hear and make the transition you remain an infant. An infant must have everything done for them. They are not weaned from milk nor are they drawn from the breast.

Imagine living your whole life never really hearing God for yourself. Instead you are dependent on others to teach you what the Bible says. I know many people who will go looking for someone who hears from God to give them guidance. While this is appropriate sometimes, why not just learn to hear from God for yourself. Imagine never being able to understand doctrine.

Imagine never discovering the methods by which God teaches and uses to communicate with spirit beings. Wow! You come into the kingdom, a new creation in Christ Jesus (spirit being) but continue to trust exclusively in the methods by which human beings learn and communicate. This is very sad: it is a recipe for living your whole spiritual life as an infant. You might be filled with the knowledge of God, but not know your ABCs, spiritually speaking.

Millions and millions of Christians live their whole time on the earth, ever learning but never coming to the knowledge of the truth, having a knowledge of God but denying the power. It happens all the time, but don't let it happen to you. Embrace the entry level operation of diversities of tongues.

Become very familiar with the kingdom and the power and the glory of God by studying the various types of tongues and becoming active in using them. This is how the power of the kingdom comes.

The Holy Spirit brings the power of God to you.

YOUR MOST HOLY FAITH

> But ye, beloved, building up yourselves on your
> most holy faith, praying in the Holy Ghost.
> Keep yourselves in the love of God, looking for
> the mercy of our Lord Jesus Christ unto eternal
> life (Jude 1:20–21).

Jude was referring to the most holy faith that exists, praying in the Holy Ghost. If you read the beginning of this book you will discover that Jude is exhorting the church to contend for "the faith that was once delivered unto the saints" (Jude 1:3). A problem entered into the church that effectively neutralized *__that kind of faith.__* Jude goes on to explain the problem which resulted from carnal men creeping into our family who were sensual, carnal, lustful, worldly… "having not the spirit."

They are described as:

1. Ungodly men: verse 4

2. Turning grace into lasciviousness: verse 4

3. Denying the only Lord God: verse 4

4. Denying our Lord Jesus Christ :verse 4

5. Filthy dreamers: verse 8

6. Defiling the flesh: verse 8

7. Despising dominion: verse 8

8. Speaking evil of dignities: verse 8

9. Sensual, having not the spirit: verse 19

When we think of these descriptions, we normally conclude that he is not talking about me or you, but of some other "evil" people. Yet go through the list and you might see these rebellious, self-willed attitudes and sins in yourself without much effort. I know I have. The list concludes and sums up this type of person...***sensual, having not the spirit.***

He is warning us of these things, then points to the kind of faith that saves us all from being like these "filthy dreamers."

What is the antidote to being ruled by the senses?

> But ye beloved, building up yourselves on your most holy faith, praying in the Holy Ghost (Jude 1:20).

Being ruled by the senses, self-willed and rebellious is how Christ found us all. As a new creation in Christ you are a spirit being. Why then would you still operate as a mere man; missing out on the REST and the REFRESHING available to those who make the transition?

There are two kinds of faith; *sense knowledge faith* that demands physical evidence that he is healed; or that he has what he has prayed for. The second kind is the *"Faith that was once delivered unto the saints,"* which Jude exhorts that we earnestly contend for.

This faith depends on the Word alone. It is confident that what God has said is true and that He is able also to perform it. Prayer based upon the Word of God rises above a sense-dominated realm and reaches the Author and Finisher of our faith. The faith that reaches God is the latter kind. Jude is instructing us to live in the realm of faith, far above the sense-ruled realm.

He knew that you only operate in that kind of faith, if you are building yourself up in your most holy faith, praying in the Holy Ghost. Prayer assisted by the Holy Ghost, not dependent upon feelings or senses, but dependent upon the Word of God, is the holiest faith there is. Operate exclusively by that kind of faith and watch strongholds crumble.

The Apostle Paul was very active in diversities of tongues. He said, I thank my God, I speak with tongues more than ye all (1 Corinthians 14:18).

The method of contending for "the Faith" is through praying in tongues. In doing so you are yielding your tongue to the Holy Ghost. It becomes an instrument of righteousness. Now God is using your tongue to pray through you, the type of prayer that changes you from the inside and brings you along into His plan for you. This is a very holy exchange. Yielding that smallest member (the tongue) as an instrument of righteousness; you are completely trusting God with your tongue. The Holy Spirit is supplying the language and He never says anything that He does not hear the Father say; He is leading you into all truth. He is in charge of your transformation process. Remember that while you pray in an unknown tongue your spirit is praying. A spirit being (you) is communicating directly to God, who is also a Spirit, in the language God chose for spiritual communication.

You can trust Him to pray exactly what is needed to lift you up above the sense-ruled, sense-dominated realm of the flesh, into the "Amen Realm" the realm that only agrees with the Word of God. The Spirit and the Word agree. Agreement with heaven gets the job done, every time. This is the kind of faith that the early Apostles had and by which they taught the early saints to walk. They spoke the Word of God and knew the authority that they had been given in the Name of Jesus. They had faith in that Name. Miracles happened because they used that Name. People's lives were spared through that Name. **The revelatory connection to the power came through the revelation gift of diversities of tongues.**

Isaiah prophesied about this transition: conversion to the new programing of those ruled by the spirit within, subject to the only Lord God and to our Lord Jesus Christ.

Missing the transition had a consequence. To the ones who failed to adopt the transition he writes:

But the word of the LORD was unto them precept upon precept, precept upon precept; line
upon line, line upon line; here a little, *and* there
a little; *that they might go, and fall backward, and
be broken, and snared, and taken* (Isaiah 28:13,
italics mine).

Going and falling backward, broken, snared and taken does
not sound at all pleasant. But this has been the fate of millions
who have *resisted the way* God has established. Only by walking in the way, the truth and the life are you free. Knowing
about religious things falls miserably short of experiencing
them as reality in this life.

*Let us therefore fear, lest, a promise being left us of
entering into his rest, any of you should seem to come
short of it.* For unto us was the gospel preached,
as well as unto them: but the word preached
did not profit them, *not being mixed with faith in
them that heard it.* For we which have believed do
enter into rest, as he said, As I have sworn in my
wrath, if they shall enter into my rest: although
the works were finished from the foundation of
the world (Hebrews 4:1–3, italics mine).

For *he that is entered into his rest, he also hath
ceased from his own works*, as God *did* from his.
Let us labour therefore to enter into that rest,
lest any *man fall after the same example of unbelief*
(Hebrews 4:10–11, italics mine).

Take heed, brethren, lest there be in any of you
an evil heart of unbelief, in departing from the
living God (Hebrews 3:12).

Doing the kingdom as the King designed it is the only way. Doing otherwise is departing from the living God. In a kingdom of action idleness equals deception.

Studying Karate without Ever Doing Karate

"I know Karate."

"How long have you been using Karate?"

"I didn't say I was using Karate, just that I know Karate."

"Oh really....then you don't KNOW Karate; You only know about Karate?"

"Are you saying I don't really know Karate unless I practice Karate? I have read so much about Karate."

"That's right, Karate is a way of Life, it is a discipline. You must study and you must train. Training is very hard and requires commitment and discipline. You will suffer as you train. You will spend hours in physical exercises, learning technics, practicing them over and over again, then using them in competition against others who are equally committed and hard working. Are you sure you want to KNOW Karate?"

"No I don't think I would, the cost seems too high."

"Yes the cost is very high."

Studying Christianity
without Ever Doing Christianity

"I am a Christian."

"How long have you been a Christian?"

"Two years now."

"How often do you pray?"

"I don't."

"Have you been baptized?"

"No."

"Do you read the Bible?"

"No."

"Do you pray for the sick?"

"No."

Do you pray in tongues?

"No."

"Do you lead others to Christ?"

"Do you cast out devils?"

"NO and NO…"

"Then what do you do?"

"I do whatever I want to do."

"What do you mean by that?"

"I am just like everybody else…Whatever I feel like doing that's what I do."

"So you do what you want whenever you feel like it?"

"Yes I do."

"Then you are not a Christian, you only know about Christ."

"What? How can you say that?"

"Because a Christian is not known for what he says and might believe he knows, but through what he does."

"Please explain."

"Sure…believing is evidenced by what you are doing. Christianity is a way of Life. When a man believes in Christ, he is born again, but it does not end there. He becomes part of a family. The family of God is part of a new creation of spirit beings. The old man that you were, has been declared dead, and the old life you had is now finished.

*Your new life is in a new family. Its operations, or way of life is vastly different, because it is life lived as a different class of being, the God class. We are no longer "like everybody else." We are now sons of God and take on the nature of our Father in heaven. As His children the life that we now live is lived in Christ. We have duties to perform, like presenting our bodies to Him as a living sacrifice, holy and acceptable to God; not conforming to the world, their attitudes and behaviors, but becoming transformed by the renewing of our minds, praying, studying and reading the word then doing what it says, so that our **actions prove that we are doing the will of God**… We also heal the sick, casting out devils, sharing our beliefs and activities with those who have yet to believe. We must still be active in the world, but we are not part of it. We must dedicate our time, energy and resources to the family business, the business of doing what our Lord Jesus instructs us to do."*

"Aren't you just a religious fanatic?"

"No but you are…"

"Why do you say that?"

"Because you live according to a "Christianity" you have made for yourself, in your own mind. You do exactly what you want. You are your own god." Jesus is not the truth, the way or

the life to you, you would rather live a lie." Calling yourself a Christian without showing the Biblical fruit is not reality."

"I see your point. It sounds like being a Christian carries a high cost. I must give up my old ways of thinking and doing my own thing if I am to be a true Christian."

"Yes, it will cost you. You must become a disciple. You must train and exercise what you have been taught and do the works that you have been assigned to do by God. That way you can walk in the truth.

There is much to learn but you must choose to become a disciple and live this life as a daily reality. He gives authority to His servants, and to every man His work...He has work for you to do."

> *For the Son of man is* as a man taking a far journey, who left his house, *and gave authority to his servants, and to every man his work,* and commanded the porter to watch (Mark 13:34, italics mine).

"Thank you for giving it to me straight...I see where I have been living a lie, I don't want to continue the way I have been . . . Can I change?"

"Yes you can and you must give yourself completely to God.

"OK I will."

"What if doing so would require many hours in prayer?"

"By the grace of God I will. Would you show me what to do? I will do it. I want to walk in the truth."

"Yes I will, teaching others is also part of walking in the truth."

THE HOLY SPIRIT WILL LEAD US INTO ALL TRUTH.

The Holy Spirit supplies the language. He also knows exactly how you fit into the eternal plan of God. His job is to build you up in these core competencies so that you become very useful to the family business. When you grow and pass the tests along the way, you will advance in the kingdom and get even more grace. You will be able to do more and with greater efficiency because you have mastered hearing from God, building yourself up on your most holy faith, speaking mysteries and operating in other gifts as the Holy Spirit adds them to you.

Is there an order to advancement in the kingdom, similar to the way a person might advance in a corporation? Yes there is.

As you may have guessed, diversities of tongues is the entry-level gift. It is the mail room, the communication department. It is the engine that drives all other gifts and levels of advancement. You must maintain the fundamentals throughout the process of advancement. To do otherwise is to impede your progress. Forget the fundamentals and you don't progress until you get back to the basics. But remember them, reapply them and you are back in the game.

Here is the Model of Advancement in the Kingdom.

> And God hath set some in the church, first apostles, secondarily prophets, thirdly teachers, after that miracles, then gifts of healings, helps, governments, diversities of tongues (I Corinthians 12:28).

The order goes from the architects, (apostles) visionaries, (prophets) instructors, (teachers) miracles, (evangelist) gifts of healings (pastor), helps, governments, and diversities of tongues. In the above scripture the order comes from the top (apostle) and goes down all the way to the entry level operation (diversities of tongues). All of us start at the entry level, at the bottom. (We will explore these operations of God more fully in the next chapter).

If we stay in the qualifying processes we add to our basic skill-sets and advance into the higher levels. Those who advance turn around and teach others. When we teach others we are more useful and bring others higher. These gifts and skillsets are part of **the operations of God** (the family business).

He designed them so that we can become fruitful. Believers who aren't producing fruit are not happy. They may not be aware of why, but you can be sure, they are not functioning according to God's design. The way to contentment as a new creature **is integration into the family and into the operations of God**. We are only happy when we are making a difference according to our design.

Function and production satisfy our basic need to leave a legacy. Unless we are making a difference around us, we are not satisfied. This is how we were designed.

My friend Ryan came to me one year. He was disillusioned in his walk with God; did not like his life and was very miserable. He told me how he was feeling and asked if I thought I could help him. I saw that he was very serious so I took him on as a student. The one condition was that he do what I tell him to do. He agreed.

I knew he worked in a meat processing plant and used his hands all day touching meat. So I told him to look at his hands and repeat after me. "When these hands touch meat, I am a praying machine." He repeated it. I asked him to say it over and over, because I wanted him to accept deep within himself that he would pray every time his hands touched a piece of meat. He agreed that he would accept the lifestyle of praying in other tongues while at work, if that's what it took.

If he did not do as I said, he understood that his choice was evidence that he did not really want to change and that I would not work with him.

So the next day he went to work. It was a struggle to pray in tongues that day and it did not get any easier the second day or the third. But he began to get used to it and was faithful. He was committed and willing to take action.

Ryan kept track of the hours he prayed in other tongues and was praying five hours a day. This turned into weeks and then into months of regular prayer. Within a couple of months his world at work began to change. Instead of thinking negative, defeated thoughts, his thoughts were redirected toward the kingdom of God. He began thinking about raising the dead, emptying hospitals and evangelizing the world. I did not put these ideas into his head. They were not on his radar when he began praying in other tongues, but he received them as he fellowshipped with God.

Ryan had times that he hit a wall in prayer and felt like he could not continue, but the Holy Spirit would remind him of his desire to change and that's all it took for him to continue. During one of these walls that he was hitting, I was thinking about him when the Lord gave me a revelation about what Ryan had been doing in prayer.

He said that he was applying the wax on/wax off principle. I understood the reference having seen Karate kid. So I told Ryan what the Holy Spirit had shown me. Ryan was mastering the elementary movements of the kingdom of God. God was transforming Ryan through diversities of tongues into the champion He had created him to be. If he had not stepped into the entry level gifting he would have stayed miserable. Instead, within five months he started talking about going to Africa with me on my mission trip. I thought it might just be wishful thinking, but he kept saying he wanted to go, so we came up with a plan and he went.

By the time we went to Africa he had already prayed for over 700 hours in other tongues. It was a real stretch for him and he was put to the test many times, but he cast out devils, healed the sick and performed miracles. A woman he prayed for was healed of AIDS. Several were healed of malaria and fevers of all kinds. Others received new hearts. We even prayed to raise a man from the dead. He did not rise from the dead, but that does not matter. Ryan had already advanced from diversities of tongues and began operating in governments, helps, gifts of healings and working of miracles. Not bad for a man who was miserable seven months before. Who knew there was so much promise for Ryan? I sure didn't. But God has this plan for all of His children.

We affectionately refer to this process as "working the plan." Thank God "the plan" is idiot proof. Not even I can screw it up. Ryan and I rejoice over this and laugh about this plan being idiot proof. Ryan just texted me 20 minutes ago to tell me he just passed the 2100 hour level. In the past two years he has put in 2100 hours in diversities of tongues. Yes, the plan is idiot-proof, anyone can do it. Anyone can hear from God.

After coming back from Africa, Ryan began having meetings in a heavenly "board room." At work he would pray in other tongues and have encounters where he had meetings with the Godhead. The Father, Son and Holy Spirit would meet with him. As he prayed God would stick His finger out of a cloud and point to an angel; the angel would be dispatched at lightning speed to go and perform what He was sent to do.

Ryan began to understand that he was partnering with heaven to bring to pass the purposes of God on the earth. He would pray and have real encounters with God. He started experiencing peace like he had never known and staying in God's presence for hours at a time. He is progressing nicely and I expect great reports from him in the future.

One thing really stands out as far as Ryan is concerned. **Before our conversation he really did not know what he was doing wrong, because he was never taught**. But when he was instructed in the kingdom, he embraced his personal responsibility for his own development and has not looked back since. Now that he has been awakened to the kingdom and found the path of light, he could never be satisfied to go back to sleep spiritually and neither will you.

Ryan is just like you…he is not happy unless he is producing fruit.

I thank God for the revelation he has given me. It has all come from the entry-level operation of diversities of tongues. This book is a result of my "working the plan" for myself.

Get in that mail room and develop those core competencies of **hearing God, receiving revelation and obeying His commands**. The sooner you decide to put in the work the sooner you advance in the kingdom. Believe me; it is amazing to walk in the spirit. When you walk in the spirit as a productive son, you are satisfied and you get to participate in miracles. How cool is that?

6

THE MASTER'S WHEEL

This is called a training circle, a master's wheel. This circle will be your world, your whole life. Until I tell you otherwise, there is nothing outside of it.

~ Diego de la Vega (*The Mask of Zorro*)

I n this scene of the movie, Diego de la Vega (Zorro) takes on a student who wishes to become a skilled swordsman. Zorro introduces his young protégé Alejandro Murrietta to the training circle, a master's wheel. ***This 200 square foot space is the place where a man with a sword, becomes a sword master.***

The young man is undisciplined, impulsive, given to anger and is an alcoholic, any of which would be an advantage to a skilled adversary with a sword. In order to become a skilled warrior, he must submit himself entirely to the elder master and overcome his disadvantages if he is to have any hope of beating his enemy.

Zorro sets the parameters of Alejandro's world in the training circle. He must remain there, completely immersed in his lessons until the master says he is ready. He tells Alejandro that this circle will be his whole world, his whole life and until the master says otherwise, nothing exists outside of it.

Alejandro must now submit to the master without question, and his whole focus must be on his training. To do this he must master himself. Personal discipline must be accomplished; a discipline that is honed through hard work, having faith in the outcome and patience in the journey.

The first lessons are very basic and become progressively more difficult as Alejandro must deal with his character flaws, which, thus far have limited him in life. These flaws get worked out as the commitment and discipline to greatness overtake these limitations.

Within the master's wheel only the student and the teacher exist. Nothing exists outside of the circle.

Any man can swing a sword. To an adversary less skilled than you, you might even win a few fights. But there will come a day when you happen upon an enemy who is a master swordsman. On that day you will be easily defeated; and in sword fighting, "that day" is the day you lose your life. Alejandro realized that to win he had to become the best; so he did. What he did not know going into his training was that all his discipline would result in a very profound and joyous reality.

> *You will become like the one*
> *with whom you spend the most time.*

The legendary Zorro was a man who cared deeply for his people. He was a hero in the eyes of his people because of the heroic and selfless ways in which he fought against evil men who oppressed and manipulated the poor for their own greedy purposes.

Young Alejandro began his quest to avenge his brother's killer, but in the end he became the next Zorro; a liberator of his people. He took on the heart of the master.

Similarly God has called you to enter the master's wheel. This training circle is the place where the Holy Ghost becomes your master. God set the whole thing up for you so that you will become a champion within the kingdom of light. Motivations vary, person to person, as to why you may wish to be a champion, yet when you spend time with God, you are changed. As the flaws within become healed and your heart is touched by His love, you too see His people, your people, through His sight. You then lead others to the light.

He has given you a sword, the Word of God and He has also given you a teacher, the Holy Ghost. It is the Holy Ghost who has received the mandate to instruct you in the use of your sword. Like Alejandro, you must be willing to give up the world as you have known it in order to become a champion. Your teacher is the one who develops the lesson plan. Your teacher is the one who defines your new existence and the boundaries in which He will train you.

As the student you must submit to the training and discipline of the teacher. You must be willing to give up all rights to personal autonomy and yield to the command of the teacher. The more willingly you surrender, the more productive your time spent in training will be.

From the moment you are birthed into the family of God the Holy Ghost is assigned to you. From the time you come to Christ until the time you leave the earth, He is your teacher; your instructor in all things related to the kingdom and to the realm of the Spirit.

It is for this reason that you must develop an absolute loyalty and obedience to the teacher. In time your complete attention and delight in His instruction will become automatic. He will become your greatest resource and beloved companion.

He will remind you of everything Jesus has spoken to you.

He will comfort you.

> But the Comforter, *which is* the Holy Ghost,
> whom the Father will send in my name, he shall
> teach you all things, and bring all things to your
> remembrance, whatsoever I have said unto you
> (John 14:26).

He will take all things that have been given to Christ and
He will show them to you.

> Howbeit when he, the Spirit of truth, is come,
> he will guide you into all truth: for he shall not
> speak of himself; but whatsoever he shall hear,
> *that* shall he speak: and he will shew you things
> to come (John 16:13).

He will only tell you what He hears the Father saying. He
will show you things to come. The revelation streams of the
Holy Ghost are absolutely pure. Impurities do not exist in Him.
He is absolutely holy.

He is perfect and He is powerful. To obey Him is to gain
access to your entire inheritance as a saint in light.

He will teach you to pray and will join in prayer with you.
When you are stuck and don't know what to pray as you should
He will help your inabilities to produce results and develop you
beyond all handicaps. He will intercede for you according to
the master blueprint of your personal callings. He has that plan
within Him and knows exactly how you fit into God's blueprint
within the Body of Christ. He will place you exactly where you
belong (Romans 8:26–28).

If you stay committed to His processes, all things will work
together for your good, because submission to Him is the sign
that you love God and that you are called according to His purposes. Stay with His process and you will be conformed to the

image of God's Son, as He has predestined you to do (Romans 8:29). It was ordained before the foundation of the world. Nothing will be able to separate you from the love of God. His love has been shed abroad and resides in your heart because the teacher is in you, the love of God came with Him.

He will not teach you by using the words that man's wisdom teaches; you will learn from Him in the manner with which He teaches, comparing spiritual things with spiritual (see 1 Corinthians 2:13). He does not want your confidence to be in the wisdom of men, but in the power of God. So you must learn to embrace the power of God and the hope of glory within you to do the works of Jesus. This is all part of your preparation.

He will guide you through your inward man, "the hidden man of the heart." God will light the candle within, illuminating your understanding (Proverbs 20:27). He will open the scriptures to you. This suggests that understanding scripture cannot be done without His assistance. You would be right to assume this. The scriptures are not made alive by your intellect, so to depend exclusively on your intellect is a fool's game. Alejandro could not teach himself, but needed the master. You will come to understand your dependence upon the Holy Spirit as well. Jesus knew this and proclaimed that when the Holy Spirit came, you would do the same works that He did, provided you believe. After all Jesus depended entirely on the Holy Spirit to guide Him in His ministry.

The Holy Ghost, your personal instructor, will open the scriptures. He will illuminate your spirit and lead you internally by your spirit, for your teacher, the Holy Ghost, lives on the inside of your spirit.

You have this treasure in your earthen vessel so that the excellency of the power might be of God and not of you, for you must know, that all men must be pointed to the Father through his Son Jesus Christ. They must place their confidence also in the demonstration of the power of God, not in words fashioned by the intellect.

His teaching includes a spiritual language that He will give to you. Through this language your inward man will talk to God and through this language God will talk to you. A new method of learning will unfold to you. Sons of God are not human beings, but spirit beings living in a temple (the body) of the Holy Ghost. We are revelatory by nature, and revelation is gained through the spirit. So God will use a new spiritual method to train you.

As a disciple, the Holy Ghost will share secrets and mysteries with you. The mysteries will become keys that will open kingdom gates and doors, and will shut doors and gates that you have been assigned to keep watch over. These mysteries will carry great authority, and will be a part of you at all times. When you discover secret things that have been hidden, those things become yours.

> The secret *things belong* unto the LORD our God:
> but those *things which are* revealed *belong* unto us
> and to our children for ever, that *we* may do all
> the words of this law (Deuteronomy 29:29).

This authority is delivered within another mystery, the mystery of the anointing of your teacher. Those He instructs He empowers to do good works and to heal all those who are oppressed of the devil, because He is God and He is with you.

Greater is He that is within you, than He that is in the world (1 John 4:4). You see, your adversary, is no match for your master, but your masters' job is to see to it, that your adversary is no match for you. God has chosen His church to reveal His manifold wisdom to the principalities and powers in heavenly places. He has chosen the weak things of this world to confound those things that are mighty, so he placed the mighty one within you. He came not to bring peace but a sword.

He will purge the character flaws from your life. He will prepare you for the day that you will meet Jesus face to face. When that day comes, you will already know Jesus, because your teacher has revealed Him to you in a way your intellect never could. On that day you will marvel, because you will be like Him. Your teacher will groom you and prepare you as you are changed into the image of Jesus Christ from glory to glory. He will instruct you in righteousness and true holiness.

You would think it would be enough to assign an angel to instruct you in such things, but our extravagant Father God sent the very best; The Spirit of Truth. Who better to guide you into all truth?

Take up your sword and enter the master's wheel. It will be the best thing you have ever done. I promise you. Call on the Holy Ghost right now. Ask Him to draw you into the secret chambers that house your personal training wheel. When you emerge you will be just like Jesus, the Master of all sword masters.

Shall we begin?

Separation

Alejandro had to be separated *from the world* he knew and *separated unto the training and discipline of his master.*

> Paul, a servant of Jesus Christ, called *to be* an apostle, *separated unto* the gospel of God (Romans 1:1, italics mine)

Many of us are called, but few are ever separated. The first separation is the new creation separating from the old life. The Word of God is then built into us as we are separated unto the gospel of Christ. Next we make individual choices to separate ourselves from things that are not sinful, but are unnecessary because of our calling. Each year this separation continues until the world has lost its dominion over us. We get freer from those things that once had a hold upon us and we become more separated unto the work that we have been given to do. This separation brings us fully into the spiritual operations of the kingdom enabling us to become extremely fruitful.

En Garde!

My son, attend to my words; incline thine ear unto my sayings. Let them not depart from thine eyes; keep them in the midst of thine heart. For they *are* life unto those that find them, and health to all their flesh. Keep thy heart with all diligence; for out of it *are* the issues of life. Put away from thee a froward mouth, and perverse lips put far from thee. Let thine eyes look right on, and let thine eyelids look straight before thee. Ponder the path of thy feet, and let all thy ways be established. Turn not to the right hand nor to the left: remove thy foot from evil (Proverbs 4:20–27).

En Garde is a term used in fencing. It is French for "on your guard." Two swordsmen take their positions completely focused, highly alert and ready to do battle. Preparation has been made; they are ready to fight. Often time they are required to fight to the death.

God has given us everything that is required to prepare ourselves in the Word of God. In Proverbs 4:20 His first instruction is to call us to attention.

I spent three years in the military. I started my training at the bottom in basic training. Basic training is designed to take ordinary young people, separate them from everything they have known and transform them into soldiers in only six weeks. The first understanding you must come to is that the drill instructor is in charge of you. No matter where you came from, what your position was in society or who you daddy is, none of that matters; the drill instructor has complete authority over you … period.

He will tell you when to get up, when you eat: every move you make has already been planned and you have no say anymore.

When the drill instructor yells "attention" you stop what you are doing, you snap to attention, stand erect, eyes facing straight ahead, frozen in place. You are not to utter a sound; you are to listen intently to whatever follows. This is the first command you learn.

This is what is meant in Proverbs 4:20 "My son attend to my words." You stop whatever it is you are doing and your ears focus on listening. Our Father wishes to instruct us by using His words. By attending to His word, you receive His instruction and conduct yourself with discipline. To focus on what He says is important. The Holy Spirit is the voice of our Father to us. He is speaking what He hears the Father say. When you hear Him instructing you through the Word of God, come to attention, God is speaking to you.

Back in my military days our drill instructor was with us all the time. He was with us the whole day. Sometimes we grew weary of hearing his voice, but that was part of learning to obey; you had to obey when you wanted to and when you didn't. And over the period of six weeks you learned the basics of being a soldier. Our instruction included what to do with our weapons. We learned to maintain them and had regular training using them, so we became very adept in the use of our weapons.

We trained in pressure situations called 'live fire training' so that we were familiar with the sounds and sights of war. It is in the pressure situations that your training benefits you the most. Through your training you are able to maintain focus on the orders you receive until the mission is successful;

performing under pressure and in times of hardship becomes second nature when you have trained for it. At times you were pushed past your breaking point. At this point you discover that you are capable of much more than you thought you could bear and that there was another gear you did not know you had.

We practiced basic things over and over and over and over. They became second nature. Through drills and exercises we mastered basic competencies. Rarely was someone required to repeat basic training, but it happened once in a while. The reason it was rare is because it is nearly impossible to do something over and over for six weeks and not become reasonably competent, even in stress-filled situations. Being pushed past your limits makes you aware that you are capable of far more than you imagined.

In the kingdom of God attending to His word, receiving His instructions, keeping them as the apple of your eye, knowing that your Father loves you and wants to equip and protect you as you prepare to do His works are keys to becoming competent. It is a battle. But if you win the battle over wanting your own way, doing your own thing, choosing a life of your own making, you will be prepared unto every good work and become very skillful in the use of your weapons.

In Proverbs 4:20–27 the Holy Spirit instructs us through the Word of God to apply:

1. Our attention to His words.

2. Our ears listening for His words.

3. Our eyes, as we keep His word before them.

4. Our heart, life gushes and flows from us from within our hearts. If we embrace His words with our heart as a reservoir, there will always be an abundance of life flowing out from it.

5. Our mouth and our lips. Removing from our lips any perverseness.

6. Our focus, eyes looking straight before us with a discipline so complete that our eyelids are in agreement.

7. Our feet, removing them from evil paths, and bringing us into harmony with God's ways. His paths, walking in the way of His instruction.

These instructions have a purpose … to walk away *from* destructive ways and *towards* fruitfulness.

When you look at this passage it is easy to remember the military instruction, which is designed to forge a new way of operating that produces soldiers and champions. The commands of the Lord when followed without question transform you into a highly trained and motivated disciple who is becoming more like your Father every day. You are learning His ways, following in His footsteps, speaking right things and conducting yourself in the Spirit, with excellence.

A Reasonable Service

I beseech you therefore, brethren, by the mercies of God, that ye present your bodies a living sacrifice, holy, acceptable unto God, *which is* your reasonable service. And be not conformed to this world: but be ye transformed by the renewing of your mind, that ye may prove what *is* that good, and acceptable, and perfect, will of God. For I say, through the grace given unto me, to every man that is among you, not to think *of himself* more highly than he ought to think; but to think soberly, according as God

hath dealt to every man the measure of faith
(Romans 12:1–3).

Proverbs 4:20–27 is a picture of Romans 12:1–3
We have all been given the measure of faith to present our
bodies. We are directed away from aimless paths of conforming
to the world, into transformation. Transformation is our ulti-
mate purpose. This also is separation from the world.

Following Jesus as a true disciple is not an easy thing for
the flesh. We must present our entire self to His processes. We
must be willing to enter the master's wheel. Our training circle
is a realm we enter into that will change us. It will remove us
from the entrapments and vanities of the world systems and
transform us to have the mind of Christ.

**Again, these instructions have a purpose…to walk away
from destructive ways and *towards* fruitfulness.**

As our minds are renewed and conformed to the mind of
Christ the grace that is given to us to go through this process
enables us **to advance**. More specialized training and advanced
missions become possible because the core competencies
learned in basic training build the foundation for exploits.

> And such as do wickedly against the covenant
> shall he corrupt by flatteries: but the people
> that do know their God shall be strong, and do
> *exploits* (Daniel 11:32).

This passage from Daniel is about soldiers in the last times.
Those operating outside of the covenant and its practices will
be corrupted by flatteries, however those who have come into
the training circle and intimately know their God, will become
stronger and do exploits.

In this war that rages for the souls of men, knowing God
through presenting your body to Him and yielding to the
transformation process is the developmental platform by which

soldiers are prepared. If you will perform your reasonable service, the developmental process guarantees your success. Why is that? Because it is the model that God designed for us to follow and success is guaranteed because of the measure of faith that God has deposited in each one of us. That measure is more than enough to develop you as a competent, skillful warrior.

In the military, everything that is needed: uniforms, weapons, etc., to do your job are supplied. The same thing is true in the army of God. His grace is in ample supply, and yielding to Him engages the grace.

The Vine

I am the true vine, and my Father is the husbandman. Every branch in me that beareth not fruit he taketh away: and every *branch* that beareth fruit, he purgeth it, that it may bring forth more fruit. Now ye are clean through the word which I have spoken unto you. Abide in me, and I in you. As the branch cannot bear fruit of itself, except it abide in the vine; no more can ye, except ye abide in me. I am the vine, ye *are* the branches: He that abideth in me, and I in him, the same bringeth forth much fruit: for without me ye can do nothing. If a man abide not in me, he is cast forth as a branch, and is withered; and men gather them, and cast *them* into the fire, and they are burned. If ye abide in me, and my words abide in you, ye shall ask what ye will, and it shall be done unto you. Herein is my Father glorified, that ye bear much fruit; so shall ye be my disciples (John 15: 1–8).

Fruitfulness cannot exist except you abide in the vine. The vine is Jesus Christ. Abiding means to continue in His Word and follow His example. The Holy Spirit is your connection to Jesus. He reminds you of everything Jesus says to you. By hearing His instruction and obeying Him we abide in the True Vine. The True Vine is the only vine that the Holy Spirit opens to you. The Holy Spirit is the Spirit of truth. He has no other objective than for you to abide in the True Vine. Abiding in Him is the only source of life.

> But ye have an unction from the Holy One, and ye know all things (1 John 2:20).

> But the anointing which ye have received of him abideth in you, and ye need not that any man teach you: but as the same anointing teacheth you of all things, and is truth, and is no lie, and even as it hath taught you, ye shall abide in him (1 John 2:27).

Because the anointing of the Holy Ghost abides within you, you are able to abide in Christ. The anointing of the Holy Ghost is your connection to Jesus.

The anointing and the unction of the Holy Ghost teach you and make you competent in the realm of the Spirit. Everything you need to know to abide in Him and receive truth is found in Him. He is your direct connection to Jesus and to the Father, fellowship with the Father and with His Son is found in His Spirit; the life within the vine reaches your spirit because of this anointing. It is the trump card or Rosetta Stone for any situation you will face. At times you may feel forsaken by others but you are never left to stand alone. The Holy Spirit is ever present and never leaves you. We can do nothing by ourselves. Dependency upon the Holy Ghost and attachment to the True Vine provides the grace of God. Grace and truth, mingled together produce fruit. As we begin to produce fruit our Heavenly Father purges us so that we may bring forth even more fruit.

In the military, when a soldier makes it through basic training, he begins to specialize. He might go into the infantry, communications, Special Forces, airborne, Navy Seals, etc. Each level of training builds upon the basic training. Each level of training has its suffering and its difficulties, yet you adapt and grow while you train. Advanced training brings the soldier to higher levels of competency. He becomes useful in a greater number of ways. He is able to be used in missions that require the various skills he has. The greater the skills and experience he has; the more useful he becomes.

As soon as he is fruitful in one way, he goes back into training so that he can become more fruitful. Our Father, the vine dresser, takes branches bearing fruit and he purges them so that they will produce more fruit.

He continually puts you into situations that stretch you and build within you a greater capacity for both revelation (training) and experience (deployment). The more missions you take part in the more God trains you. There is an ever increasing competency…an ever increasing faith.

Promotion

For promotion *cometh* neither from the east, nor from the west, nor from the south. But God *is* the judge: he putteth down one, and setteth up another (Psalm 75:6–7).

In the previous chapter "The Mail Room" we talked about the entry level operation of diversities of tongues. Like children at play, building blocks are fundamental to creativity and learning. Praying in tongues is a developmental exercise that causes the inner man to be built up and on alert. All believers are called to this kind prayer because it activates all resources and spiritual abilities resident within the kingdom of God. When you become operationally competent, you are called to build upon what you have achieved through training and experience, adding to what you already have. Praying in other tongues will always be a part of everything you will do within this spiritual kingdom. So get used to praying a lot in other tongues. Think of it as keeping your motor running. Pray continually.

> Praying *always* with all prayer and supplication *in the Spirit*, and watching thereunto with all perseverance and supplication for all saints (Ephesians 6:18).

Governments

> And God hath set some in the church, first apostles, secondarily prophets, thirdly teachers, after that miracles, then gifts of healings, helps, governments, diversities of tongues. *Are* all apostles? *are* all prophets? *are* all teachers? *are* all workers of miracles? Have all the gifts of healing? do all speak with tongues? do all interpret? (1 Corinthians 12:28–30).

The Greek word for governments is: **koo-ber'-nay-sis** which is derived from **kubernaō** (of Latin origin, **to steer**); **pilotage, that is, (figuratively) directorship (in the church): government.**

Our first lesson in governments is found in the inward man. The inward man, through the fruit of self-control and discipline takes dominion over the desires of the flesh and of the mind. This self-control or self-government forms the foundation of governments within you. We have a mandate to first bring ourselves under the control of the inner man, with the assistance of the Holy Spirit. We have been given the measure of faith to do this through presenting our bodies to God, and through praying in other tongues. As we gain competency we begin to see that authority is released to us.

A soldier has authority, which is referred to as his rank. He has power and the skill sets in the use of weapons and matters pertaining to war. When you carry a rank you are authorized to operate at the level of your ranking, and are able to give orders based on that level of authority. As you will see, the higher you go in authority, the greater the power. But you will also understand that the entry level gift of diversities of tongues is not given to you solely for your personal development. Some tongues are for ministering to others or ministry gifts, such as speaking in tongues and interpretation of tongues. Tongues that edify self are for self-government. Tongues that bring edification to the church are for body government for the whole church.

Self-government vs. Body government

> Are all apostles? are all prophets? are all teachers? are all workers of miracles? Have all the gifts of healing? do all speak with tongues? do all interpret? (1 Corinthians 12:29–30)

Here Paul is addressing the topic of body government. He is asking whether all are operational *in body government*. **He is not asking whether all are operational in self-government**. The self-governing aspects of diversities of tongues, like praying in the Holy Ghost, speaking mysteries, personal edification and tongues for revelation, weren't included in the list; only two kinds of tongues were mentioned, spoken tongues and interpretation of tongues (the equivalent of prophesy) which are operational gifts for **Body Ministry (Body Government)**.

He goes on to suggest that we covet earnestly the best gifts, meaning the gifts that are used in ministering to the body. Our first responsibility is self-government, but as we are faithful to engage in self-government, we are also designed to engage in ministry operations which edify others.

The Corinthian church operated in many of the gifts of the spirit and yet they were called babes who were not ready to receive meat. They were self-absorbed. They were still thinking more about themselves than edifying the body. Paul's desire was that they exhibit the signs of true disciples by loving one another.

Instead the church was known for divisions, hero worship, suing one another in the courts amongst unbelievers. One man was sleeping with his father's wife. Paul's exhortations were meant to redirect them into loving one another and in being a body that edifies itself in love. They were operating in many spiritual things, but they were not being steered by God in all things. They were trapped in carnality.

The core competencies of "**body**" government are found in the operations of apostles, prophets, teachers, miracles, gifts of healings, helps, governments and diversities of tongues. These gifts enable us to edify the church and not just ourselves.

There is never any shortage of opportunities to **minister to others** within the **body** governments, yet not everyone looks to serve their brothers and sisters. Many were called in the Corinthian church, but not many had been chosen or set aside to these ministry gifts because they still fell for the dumb idols; the worst of which was idolizing their own lusts and opinions above the spiritual operations. They lost sight of the fact that the greatest of all, serves others, or **body** ministry.

Paul's purpose, in this letter, was to redirect them to loving one another and to understand that there is a purpose beyond selfishness. Their purpose as believers was to set their hearts on the spiritual things of God. Many today fall for the same trap.

> Now concerning spiritual *gifts*, brethren, I would not have you ignorant. Ye know that ye were Gentiles, carried away unto these dumb idols, even as ye were led (1 Corinthians 12:1–2).

He was calling them back to the basics: back to basic training. They had lost the vision, which is to desire gifts that would minister life to the body, convert the lost and edify the whole family of God. This was their calling but they had lost their way and had reverted to the dumb idols of carnality.

So you see there is always a 'hearing' and a 'doing' attached to being in the kingdom. When we receive a command to pray for the sick, it is a body command, part of the body-government. In these commands the body governmental operations are released. The command releases both the authority and the power to use His Name, the Name of Jesus, to heal. As I am faithful to self-govern and faithful to involve myself in body-government, then I am no longer a dysfunctional part of the family of God. I am developing core competencies in self-edification as well as body-edification.

Both governmental functions are learned simultaneously. We receive training but training is only functional if you are using it. It is mere head knowledge unless you are operating in it. Militarily, there is always a mission to which one is assigned. *If there is no deployment, your training serves no purpose.* You are dysfunctional, because you are not producing fruit. **Back to basic training for you . . .**

> And as *Jesus* passed by, he saw a man which was blind from *his* birth. And his disciples asked

him, saying, Master, who did sin, this man, or his parents, that he was born blind? Jesus answered, Neither hath this man sinned, nor his parents: but that the works of God should be made manifest in him. I must work the works of him that sent me, while it is day: the night cometh, when no man can work. As long as I am in the world, I am the light of the world. When he had thus spoken, he spat on the ground, and made clay of the spittle, and he anointed the eyes of the blind man with the clay. And said unto him, Go, wash in the pool of Siloam, (which is by interpretation, Sent.) He went his way therefore, and washed, and came seeing. The neighbours therefore, and they which before had seen him that he was blind, said, Is not this he that sat and begged? Some said, This is he: others *said*, He is like him: *but* he said, I am *he*. Therefore said they unto him, How were thine eyes opened? He answered and said, A man that is called Jesus made clay, and anointed mine eyes, and said unto me, Go to the pool of Siloam, and wash: and I went and washed, and I received sight. Then said they unto him, Where is he? He said, I know not.

They brought to the Pharisees him that aforetime was blind. And it was the sabbath day when Jesus made the clay, and opened his eyes. Then again the Pharisees also asked him how he had received his sight. He said unto them, He put clay upon mine eyes, and I washed, and do see. Therefore said some of the Pharisees, This man is not of God, because he keepeth not the sabbath day. Others said, How can a man that is a sinner do such miracles? And there was a division among them. They say unto the blind man again, What sayest thou of him, that he hath opened thine eyes? He said, He is a prophet. But the Jews did not believe concerning him, that he had been blind, and received his sight, until they called the parents of him that had received his sight. And they asked them, saying, Is this your son, who ye say was born blind? how then doth he now see? His parents answered them and said, We know that this is our son, and that he was born blind: But by what means he now seeth, we know not; or who hath opened his eyes, we know not: he is of age; ask him: he shall speak for himself. These *words* spake his parents, because they feared the Jews: for the Jews had agreed already, that if any man did confess that he was Christ, *he should be put out of the synagogue* (John 9:1–22, italics mine).

The parents deferred answering because they did not want to get kicked out of the church. Hmmm...

Therefore said his parents, He is of age; ask him. Then again called they the man that was blind, and said unto him, *Give God the praise: we know that this man is a sinner* (John 9:23–23, italics mine).

Notice that one who is doing the works of God is subject to scrutiny and/or rejection by religious leaders or people?

He answered and said, Whether he be a sinner *or no*, I know not: one thing I know, that, whereas I was blind, now I see. Then said they to him again, What did he to thee? how opened he thine eyes? *He answered them, I have told you already, and ye did not hear: wherefore would ye hear it again? will ye also be his disciples?* (John 9:25–27, italics mine).

That hit a nerve!

> Then they reviled him, and said, Thou art his disciple; but we are Moses' disciples. We know that God spake unto Moses: as for this fellow, we know not from whence he is (John 9:28–29).

The Pharisees were about to be schooled in reality by a man who they believed to be unqualified to speak the truth.

> The man answered and said unto them, Why herein is a marvellous thing, that ye know not from whence he is, and *yet* he hath opened mine eyes. Now we know that God heareth not sinners: but if any man be a worshipper of God, and doeth his will, him he heareth. Since the world began was it not heard that any man opened the eyes of one that was born blind. If this man were not of God, he could do nothing (John 9:30–33).

Snap! Ouch! If the veins on the Pharisees necks weren't already bulging, due to the rage they had against Jesus, they surely were now. They took great exception to being subjected to such wisdom from a "sinner."

> They answered and said unto him, Thou wast *altogether born in sins, and dost thou teach us?* And they cast him out (John 9:34, italics mine).

The clergy had a superior, self-absorbed belief, that because of their position, and all the things they had achieved and in all their education, that they were not like other men, "altogether born in sin."

This attitude is portrayed in Luke Chapter 18:

> Two men went up into the temple to pray; the one a Pharisee, and the other a publican. The Pharisee stood and prayed thus with himself, God, I thank thee, that I am not as other men are, extortioners, unjust, adulterers, or even as this publican. I fast twice in the week, I give tithes of all that I possess. And the publican, standing afar off, would not lift up so much as his eyes unto heaven, but smote upon his breast, saying, God be merciful to me a sinner. I tell you, this man went down to his house justified rather than the other: for every one that exalteth himself shall be abased; and he that humbleth himself shall be exalted (Luke 18:14, italics mine).

The publican knew he was a sinner in need of forgiveness but the Pharisee was above it all. He was the man of god in his day. The little "g" in god is not capitalized for a reason: I think you get my meaning. He was led away into serving dumb idols. He was "in charge." His ego and his false sense of security were his dumb idols.

People who have missed the purposes of their positions (serving others) are always jealous of those operating in the signs of the kingdom. They have not understood that the power of God is released when you are doing His will.

Improper understanding brings impotence and dysfunction. But when you are obedient to the governmental structures, both of the self and the body of Christ, power to operate as designed is released. You then operate in signs, wonders and miracles. This is basic training, not advanced training. Sons of

God walk in the power of God. The power is contained in acts of obedience to self-government and body-government.

The servant is the greatest of all. When one compares Jesus with the Pharisees, it is easy to see who the greatest is. Jesus was truly serving the people, doing the will of God! The Pharisees hated him because of it. *Jesus is the Master. He is the Christ, the Son of the living God…that's with a capital "G."*

Will you be a little g operator, or a BIG G operator? Destroy those dumb idols and graduate from basic training. You might as well know that people are still being kicked out of churches for exposing dysfunction, and for operating in authority given to them by God, but unsanctioned by the Pharisees of today.

The key is to just keep being an example to other believers. Don't explain yourself. Let the works you do stand as an example of how to walk in the body government. Let the works you do in your prayer closet and in your study of the Word behind closed doors, manifest openly as you love others through serving them. You can begin to do this from the first day you believe.

Those serving dumb idols don't like being told their doctrines stink. Jesus ran into this almost daily. He was getting attention and so will you when signs of your training begin to manifest in you in authority and power. You too will do the works He said you would.

Praise the Name of Jesus! Thank God "He has hidden these things from the wise and prudent and has revealed them unto babes, for so it seemed good in his sight" (Matthew 11:25 paraphrased)

Jurisdictional Authority

Then HE called HIS twelve disciples together and gave them POWER and AUTHORITY over all demons, and to cure diseases (Luke 9:1, emphasis mine).

POWER ~ *Dunamis*:

Dunamis is best described as raw explosive power needed to get the job done. Do you need to blow something up that doesn't want to be blown up? Use dynamite. Dynamite comes from the Greek word *dunamis*.

AUTHORITY ~ *Exousia*

Exousia is a word that represents vested governmental powers. This has to do with rank and the ability to get something done, for no other reason, than you have the authority over those under you. As a new creation, all the rankings of the demonic realm, including any spirits of infirmities, sickness or diseases, are beneath the ranking of a son or a daughter of God. Therefore your jurisdictional authority over the demonic realm is absolute. There is not a single devil that out ranks any child of God. We don't have to receive or believe anything that comes from the demonic realm. In fact what we say goes. Period!

And when Jesus was entered into Capernaum, there came unto him a centurion, beseeching him, And saying, Lord, my servant lieth at home sick of the palsy, grievously tormented. And Jesus saith unto him, I will come and heal him. The centurion answered and said, Lord, I am not worthy that thou shouldest come under my roof: but speak the word only, and my servant shall be healed. For I am a man under authority, having soldiers under me: and I say to this *man*, Go, and he goeth; and to another, Come, and he cometh; and to my servant, Do this, and he doeth *it*.

When Jesus heard *it*, he marvelled, and said to them that followed, Verily I say unto you, I have not found so great faith, no, not in Israel. And I say unto you, That many shall come from the east and west, and shall sit down with Abraham, and Isaac, and Jacob, in the kingdom of heaven. But the children of the kingdom shall be cast out into outer darkness: there shall be weeping and gnashing of teeth. And Jesus said unto the centurion, Go thy way; and as thou hast believed, *so* be it done unto thee. And his servant was healed in the selfsame hour (Matthew 8:5–13).

This centurion understood the principles of *dunamis* and *exousia*. He served Rome. The average centurion commanded between 60 to 80 men. The highest authority in Rome was Caesar, and yet the centurion perceived that Jesus had a superior authority that came from God. He knew that whatever Jesus did within His authority (*exousia*), that the power to make it happen (*dunamis)* went with the authority He had been given. If Jesus said it, it would happen. That is the authority He wants you to walk in. Yes I am talking to you…the one holding this book.

Jesus was thrilled with the faith shown by the centurion. So much so, that He brought the matter of his faith to the attention of all those who were there. It was the greatest opportunity to date for Jesus to teach what it meant to have faith and Jesus publically commended the faith of this man. Jesus then told them that many will come into the fellowship of the patriarchs in the kingdom of heaven, but the children of the kingdom would be cast out into outer darkness with weeping and gnashing of teeth.

Those who miss the revelation of the governments of jurisdictional authority cannot operate in the faith that gets the job done. In fact the lack of understanding of our authority is the reason why so many experience defeat in life and do not overcome the wicked one. If you think he has more power than you do, you live beneath your ranking (*exousia*) and suffer defeat. Step up into the ranking that Jesus is sharing with his bride "all power is given to me in heaven and in earth…[and] go therefore!" Walk with Him in "all power!" When you do, unusual things happen wherever you go; just like they did for Jesus.

You may ask what the boundaries of such jurisdictional authorities are. Do they have the same weight in heaven that they do here on the earth? Yes, you carry authority in heaven. When you need extra support you ask what you will and it is done for you. The mission of bringing heaven to earth encompasses all power and authority that is required to make it happen. The understanding of our spiritual leverage as ambassadors grows when we continue to utilize our authority. Walking in authority means putting it to practical use wherever you are.

> That Christ may dwell in your hearts by faith; that ye, being rooted and grounded in love, May be *able to comprehend with all saints what is the breadth, and length, and depth, and height; And to know the love of Christ, which passeth knowledge, that ye might be filled with all the fulness of God.* Now unto him that is able to do exceeding abundantly above all that we ask or think, according to the power that worketh in us, Unto him *be* glory in the church by Christ Jesus throughout all ages, world without end. Amen (Ephesians 3:17–21, italics mine).

The revelation expands even past our ability to ask or think. Now that is some kind of latitude.

Praise the Lord.

Angelic assistance is also part of the governments of God.

> Thinkest thou that I cannot now pray to my Father, and he shall presently give me more than twelve legions of angels? (Matthew 26:53).

So it is with us. We may ask for operations of angelic hosts to carry out assignments which will aide in the work.

> But to which of the angels said he at any time, Sit on my right hand, until I make thine enemies thy footstool? Are they not all ministering spirits, sent forth to minister for them who shall be heirs of salvation? (Hebrews 1:13–14)

As an heir of salvation the ministering spirits are at my disposal; all I need do is ask.

> Behold, I give unto you power to tread on serpents and scorpions, and over all the power of the enemy: and nothing shall by any means hurt you (Luke 10:19).

> You shall tread upon the lion and the cobra, The young lion and the serpent you shall trample underfoot (Psalm 91:13).

> Yet in all these things we are more than conquerors through HIM who loved us (Romans 8:37).

> I AM HE who lives, and was dead, and behold, I am alive forevermore. Amen. And I have The Keys of Hades and of Death (Revelation 1:18).

> Now thanks be to God who always leads us in triumph in Christ, and through us diffuses the fragrance of his Knowledge in every place. For we are to God the fragrance of Christ among those who are being saved and among those who are perishing (2 Corinthians 2:14–15).

The authority comes with a spiritual fragrance of Christ. Devils become agitated when you enter a room. They realize your authority over them perhaps more than you do, and they tremble. They will do anything to discourage you from learning about and walking in this authority.

But go ahead and fight the good fight of faith. Overcome Satan with the blood of the Lamb and the word of your testimony (Revelations 12:11 paraphrased) testify continually about how God has made you more than a conqueror and how He always leads you to triumph in Christ Jesus. When you grow in your understanding of the governments of God and walk in the authority of Jesus in submission to God, you will see the devil flee. It may surprise you at first when people are healed and delivered through your authority, but just keep rejoicing that your name is written in the Lamb's book of life. Stay true to your calling to walk as He walked. I believe you will see it and possess those keys of the Kingdom. Hallelujah!

For the disciple, the Lord's government increases in both enjoyment and scope.

Of the increase of *his* government and peace *there shall be* no end, upon the throne of David, and upon his kingdom, to order it, and to establish it with judgment and with justice from henceforth even for ever. The zeal of the LORD of hosts will perform this (Isaiah 9:7).

A great confession to make is this: "of the increase of His government and peace in my life, there shall be no end, for He sits on the throne of His father David and upon His kingdom to order it with judgment and with justice from now on. He will perform this through the zeal of the Lord of hosts."

> For it is God which worketh in you both to will and to do of *his* good pleasure (Philippians 2:13).

Helps

The Greek word for **"helps"** *(antilepsis)* is translated "**relief.**"

Relief: (Taken from Noah Webster's 1828 edition of the American Dictionary of the English Language):

1. The removal, in whole or in part, of any evil that afflicts the body of mind; the removal or alleviation of pain, grief, want, care, anxiety, toil or distress, or of any thing oppressive or burdensome, by which some ease is obtained. Rest gives relief to the body when weary; the sympathy of friends affords some relief to the distressed; a loan or a gift of money to a man embarrassed may afford him a temporary relief; a complete relief from the troubles of life is never to be expected.

2. That which mitigates or removes pain, grief or other evil.

> For God *is* not unrighteous to forget your work and labour of love, which ye have shewed toward his name, in that *ye have ministered* to the saints, and do minister (Hebrews 6:10, italics mine).

Oh what a wonderful reward awaits the beautiful people who refresh the saints.

> And the next *day* we touched at Sidon. And Julius courteously entreated Paul, and gave *him* liberty to go unto his friends *to refresh himself* (Acts 27:3, italics mine).

> There were also women looking on afar off: among whom was Mary Magdalene, and Mary the mother of James the less and of Joses, and Salome; (Who also, when he was in Galilee, followed him, and *ministered unto him;*) and many other women which came up with him unto Jerusalem (Mark 15:40–41, italics mine).

> And certain women, which had been healed of evil spirits and infirmities, Mary called Magdalene, out of whom went seven devils, And Joanna the wife of Chuza Herod's steward, and Susanna, and many others, which *ministered unto him of their substance* (Luke 8:1–3, italics mine).

Jesus washed the feet of His disciples as an example of service to one another. Sometimes you have to look closely to see the ministry of helps. When you are compelled to help others, provide relief or take care of even the smallest details for someone who is doing the work of the ministry, you are operating in helps. Some things you do for others are done in secret. Behind the scenes without adulation, saints are at work helping those in need, refreshing those working for God and praying others through to victory.

Jesus had many people who did the little things for Him and His disciples. Perhaps they needed someone to wash their clothing or to buy the things they needed while they went about the Father's business. If more people operated this way, responding to the needs of others, there would be no want. Doing the work of the ministry requires provisions. For example when travelling resources are expended while no income is forthcoming, at key moments when you think you will be unable to go on, someone shows up with a solution to the problem and brings what you require. I know missionaries who do the work God has called them to do even when nobody is willing to help them. They are following Jesus and often do things that others won't, or go places that others would not dare travel. They are not interested in doing what is comfortable but only what the Lord wants them to do.

My friend Ernie Splane drove from Canada to Mexico with his wife and kids without any money in his pocket. They jumped in the car and off they went because God had told them to. Six months later they returned home. All the time they were gone, God provided along the way, through the ministry of helps. Saints were in strategic places, sometimes without knowing why. At just the right moment the provision needed by this family was there. For six months it happened just this way for them. Most people would not obey God if He told them to do this. They would simply reject the notion and miss out on an adventure of a lifetime. Ernie and his family have a memory that will last forever and a testimony that defies lack.

God has people to whom He speaks when others are in need. For some of God's people He endows them with special abilities in business or gives them ideas that generate revenue far in excess of what they require to live. Entrepreneurs whose gifting brings them fortunes are fortunes that have been earmarked for the work of the ministry.

Others have created foundations to help the poor, providing water through well digging programs, clothing and feeding programs. When you see a brother in need and you do something to help or bring relief, you are active in the ministry of helps. We can all do something. As you build these core competencies and operate in them, you are becoming useful in many ways. You are producing fruit as you grow in the grace of the Lord Jesus.

> And God hath set some in the church, first apostles, secondarily prophets, thirdly teachers, after that miracles, then gifts of healings, helps, governments, diversities of tongues (1 Corinthians 12:28).

GIFTS OF HEALINGS AND MIRACLES

When you look at the scriptures, you notice that Jesus never healed the blind the same way twice. In my experience, most of the time, I have been directed to pray in different ways for different needs. If I thought I knew what to do and did things the same way every time, I would stop listening to God.

At times I have succumbed to doing what worked last time and the results have been limited. I prayed for many people who did not get healed. I would study healing and do what I read, attempting to believe. There were healings to be sure, but when I began listening to God in the moment, the gifts of healings began to flow quite easily and the results were overwhelming. Abiding in Him and waiting for the unction of the Holy Ghost ignited the power of the True Vine.

I have learned that listening is powerful. When I listen for instructions and hear God say something to me, the success rate of healing goes way up. Gifts of healings manifest differently most of the time. What rarely changes is the laying on of hands; almost always I will put my hands on someone when ministering in the gifts of healings. I will ask God what He wants to do and wait to see what He says.

This helps me to focus, but it also says something to the one receiving the healing. It lets them know that this operation is from God and *we are looking to Him to see what expression of the gifts will take place.* People are touched by the love of God and are very happy to know that you asked Him and He answered concerning their trouble. It is very comforting to the one receiving the healing. We all wish to be touched by God. When this happens we celebrate in the love of God, because God touched one of His children.

> By stretching forth thine hand to heal; and that
> signs and wonders may be done by the name of
> thy holy child Jesus (Acts 4:30).

This scripture is powerful. If you will think about your hands being the hand of God you give the Holy Spirit the freedom to operate in any way God wishes. Sometimes a gift of healing will take place and maybe even a miracle that you did not expect or a sign or wonder. When you are stretching forth His hand, He gets to do what He wants. This is worth thinking about. Realize that every child of God is capable of healings and miracles. Focus on this and you will see mighty deliverances from diseases and troubles.

John G. Lake, the powerful missionary to South Africa, and the pioneer of what has come to be known as the healing rooms, subjected himself to scientific experimentation concerning the effects of the Holy Spirit upon the body. In "The Complete Collection of His Life Teachings," Lake gives his amazing account of this experiment.

> At one time I submitted myself to a series of ex-
> periments. It was not sufficient to know that God
> healed; I had to know how God healed. I visit-
> ed one of the great experimental institutions and
> submitted myself for a series of experiments.
>
> First, an instrument was attached to my head.
> This instrument had an indicator that would reg-
> ister the vibrations of the brain. I began to repeat

things like the 23rd Psalm to soothe the mind and reduce its vibrations to the lowest point. Then I repeated the 31st Psalm, the 35th chapter of Isaiah, the 91st Psalm, and Paul's address before Agrippa.

After this, I went into secular literature and recited Tennyson's "Charge of the Light Brigade" and finally Poe's "The Raven." As I prayed in my heart that at the psychological moment, God would anoint my soul in the Holy Spirit.

My difficulty was that while reciting, I could not keep the Spirit from coming upon me. When I finished with "The Raven," those in charge of the experiment said, "You are a phenomenon. You have a wider mental range than any human being we have ever seen." In reality, this was not so. It was because the Spirit of God kept coming upon me to such degree that I could feel the moving of the Spirit within me.

I prayed in my heart, "Lord God, if You will only let the Spirit of God come like the lightenings of God upon my soul for two seconds, I know something is going to happen that these men have never seen before.

As I recited the last lines of the poem, suddenly The Spirit of God struck me in a burst of praise and tongues. The indicator on that instrument bounded to the limit and I haven't the least idea how much further it would have gone if it had been possible. The professors said, "We have never seen anything like it!" I replied, "Gentlemen, it is the Holy Ghost."

In the second experiment, a powerful X-ray machine with microscopic attachments was connected to my head. The purpose was to see, if possible, what the action of the brain cells was. I proceeded just as in the former experiment.

First, I repeated Scriptures that were soothing those calculated to reduce the action of the cortex coils to their lowest possible register. Then I went to Scriptures which conveyed better and richer things until I reached the first chapter of John. As I began to recite this, the fires of God began to burn in my heart. Suddenly, the Spirit of God came upon me as before, and the man who was behind me touched me. It was a signal to me to keep that poise of soul until one after another could look through the instrument. Finally, when I let go, the Spirit subsided. The professors said, "Why, man, we cannot understand this, but the cortex cells expanded amazingly."

I said to them, "Gentlemen, I want you to see one more thing. Go down in your hospital and bring back a man who has inflammation in the bone. Take your instrument and attach it to his leg. Leave enough space to get my hand on his leg. You can attach it to both sides.

When the instrument was ready, I put my hand on the man's shin and prayed like Mother Etter prays: no strange prayer, but the cry of my heart to God.

I said, "God, kill the devilish disease by Your power. Let the Spirit move in him; let it live in him." Then I asked, "Gentlemen, what is taking place? They replied, "Every cell is responding."

It is so simple: The life of God comes back into the part that is afflicted; immediately the blood flows; the closed, congested cells respond; and the work is done!

Frame your expectations with this potential. See yourself as being a conduit for God. You are His child and His children are capable of anything if only they believe. This means you too. When I lay my hands on someone and truly want to know what God wants, incredible possibilities open up right then and there. I am giving Him a chance to touch someone. I want Him to accomplish everything He wishes in the moment, believing that He wants to touch people is a powerful position from which to heal.

If you wish to operate in gifts of healing and miracles, begin to seek God and ask Him to make His voice real to you in the moment. This is quite enough to get you started.

Ask someone who has more experience than you to lay hands upon you for an impartation of the gifts of healings and the working of miracles. I am telling you, they are available to you. You will do the works of Christ.

Apostles, prophets and teachers are discussed elsewhere so these operations won't be elaborated on in this chapter.

Buckle you seatbelt, you are about to see something that few have understood about the kingdom of God.

7

DOORS AND GATES

Be an opener of doors for such as come after thee.

– Ralph Waldo Emerson

I wonder if you knew that you could open doors for others. In Canada people are very polite while out in public. Everyone checks to see if they can hold open the door for those coming in behind them. It seems so automatic that you get used to it. **You play the part of a porter for those behind you.** You also get an effort-free entrance when those already entering hold a door open for you. Jesus has already gone through every door that you will ever need entry into. But once you gain entry, be of the same mind as He, being willing to guide others.

Porter: from Latin porta, a gate.

1. A man that has the charge of a door or gate; a door-keeper.

2. One who waits at the door to receive messages.

3. A carrier; a person who carries or conveys burdens for hire.

As a courtesy to others, we naturally think of those behind us, and if we are the first to approach the door we are near, we accept the role of doorkeeper. In the first definition a porter *opens and closes* whatever gate he is in charge of opening, we understand this easily.

In the second definition the porter must *wait at the door to receive messages*. These messages most likely come from the owner of the door or gate.

A carrier, the third definition, carries or conveys burdens for hire. His hire is to assume responsibility of transporting things. Another way to look at the third definition is pick-up and delivery.

Think of the kingdom of God. In John chapter 6 we find the Lord's prayer. A purpose of the prayer is that "thy kingdom come, thy will be done on earth as it is in heaven." We are commanded to carry what is in heaven, by the authority of God, to this natural realm. We carry the authority of heaven to transport heaven's realm and superimpose it here on earth.

> *We as porters carry the power, authority, and the reality of heaven, delivering it in the natural realm so that heaven is superimposed everywhere we go.*
>
> *"Thy Kingdom come; thy will be done."*

When we see someone who is sick and we realize that in heaven there is no sickness, we are recognizing a breach. There is a breach between the reality of heaven and this person's body. *As a porter, we can lead the person to the door of healing and deliver what is true in heaven into the body of this person.* We have been to the door; we have received messages and have been hired to bring the health of heaven into the person who is sick. This is the kingdom in manifestation, a porter, delivering the reality of heaven. When you realize that you have become a gateway between time and eternity, it is quite the honor.

The kingdom of darkness (sickness) collides with the kingdom of heaven (health). The only one left intact would be the kingdom of heaven. The kingdom of heaven always wins when we are connected according to His **eternal purpose**. We are His carriers of the kingdom; supernatural porters. We become the doorway that ushers heaven to earth, eternity into time. Eternity has a mighty effect upon time.

> *When a superior kingdom comes into contact with an inferior kingdom, guess which one has to yield?*

Did you know that God is looking to fill such positions? Let's look at a few scriptures about the porter's duties.

Verily, verily, I say unto you, He that entereth not by the door into the sheepfold, but climbeth up some other way, the same is a thief and a robber. But he that entereth in by the door is the shepherd of the sheep. *To him the porter openeth*; and the sheep hear his voice: and he calleth his own sheep by name, and leadeth them out. And when he putteth forth his own sheep, he goeth before them, and the sheep follow him: for they know his voice. And a stranger will they not follow, but will flee from him: for they know not the voice of strangers (John 10:1–5, italics mine).

Here we see the porter making an opening for Christ. Consider for a moment the New Testament role of opening up to Jesus. In verse 7 He is called "The Door." You have heard people pray that God would open doors for them. This is a legitimate prayer, and God answers these prayers, but change the prayer just a bit and ask God to allow you to be a porter for Him, opening doors for Him to enter into the lives of those who need Him. If you would like this; repeat the following prayer.

"Jesus, I want to open doors for You into the lives of those around me that need you. Teach me to be a porter or be a carrier of your power to right the wrongs I see around me, to super-impose the realities of heaven here in the earth. As You instruct me in Your ways of being a porter, remind me to teach others, to hold open the doors of understanding for others to also become porters for You. I want everyone to understand and become fruitful as we all partner with heaven to be carriers of Your power."

> Then said Jesus unto them again, Verily, verily, I say unto you, I am the door of the sheep (John 10:7).

> For the Son of man is as a man taking a far journey, who left his house, and gave authority to his servants, and to every man his work, *and commanded the porter to watch* (Mark 13:34, italics mine).

Jesus has given authority to His servants and to every man His work. Authority comes to those who serve Him. Every man is given work to do. We all have assignments. The porter is commanded to watch.

During my days in the U.S. Armed Forces every soldier was trained to keep watch. We had a post or assigned areas of responsibility. There were orders to be on your post at certain times, duties to perform, and protocol to follow in the event of an enemy sighting. In the military lives hang in the balance; if an enemy slips in and opens fire and kills the other soldiers it is the fault of the watchman. The value of the lives at stake is of utmost importance. If someone were to be found sleeping at their post, they were always severely punished. The message to us was 'don't let the rest of us down…our lives are in your hands, stay alert.'

> Watch ye therefore: for ye know not when the
> master of the house cometh, at even, or at mid-
> night, or at the cockcrowing, or in the morning:
> *Lest coming suddenly he find you sleeping. And what
> I say unto you I say unto all, Watch* (Mark 13:35–37,
> italics mine).

Not only is Jesus commanding the porter to watch, He is commanding *all* to watch. **Everyone has this calling to be one that keeps watch.** Others depend on you to keep watch spiritually. This can save lives. If you are alert you can take immediate actions. You can destroy the works of the enemy and defeat his plans. You have what it takes. Devils will flee from you when you understand the ministry of the porter.

PORTERS APPOINTED TO THE DOOR OF THE TABERNACLE

> And Zechariah the son of Meshelemiah *was*
> porter of the door of the tabernacle of the
> congregation. All these *which were* chosen to
> be porters in the gates *were* two hundred and
> twelve. These were reckoned by their genealogy
> in their villages, whom David and Samuel the
> seer did ordain in their set office (1 Chronicles
> 9:21–22, italics mine).

King David and the prophet (seer) Samuel ordained them in their set office.

In the change from the old covenant to the new covenant, believers in Jesus Christ are now the temple of the living God. God no longer lives in a temple or tabernacle made of hands, but His people make up His temple; He tabernacles (dwells) **within** each of us.

Psalm 24 predicted this transition.

> Lift up your heads, O ye gates; and be ye lift up, ye everlasting doors; and the King of glory shall come in. Who *is* this King of glory? The LORD strong and mighty, the LORD mighty in battle. Lift up your heads, O ye gates; even lift *them* up, ye everlasting doors; and the King of glory shall come in (Psalm 24:7–9, italics mine).

In this Psalm gates and doors are given a command to be lifted up. These gates and doors are living beings. They have heads. Just as Jesus said "I am the door of the sheep," **He calls us** gates and doors and commands that we open up so that the King of Glory can tabernacle (make His habitation) in His new house. In His new house He declares Himself to be the Lord strong and mighty, the Lord mighty in battle and the King of Glory. This description is not of the broken man on the cross but a fierce warrior King who has overcome the world and overcame death. He wants to come in to the house that God has made for him, YOU. *YOU ARE HIS HOUSE.*

> Behold, I stand at the door, and knock: *if any man hear my voice, and open the door, I will come in to him*, and will sup with him, and he with me (Revelation 3:20, italics mine).

Here Jesus Christ, the King of Glory, the Lord strong and mighty, stands at the door knocking. Do you let Him in? You are the porter in this verse and it is you who opens up to Him, to invite fellowship with the King. As we learned in the 24th Psalm, *you are the door*; it is your decision to open the door.

This is the first duty of a porter, **to open the door every time the king comes knocking**. "To Him the porter openeth."

To open the door is to have fellowship with the One who has overcome and has sat down with His Father in His throne. We gain an advantage when we open the door, Jesus comes in. We sup with Him and He with us. In so doing we share fellowship *with the One who has already overcome.*

> To him that overcometh will I grant to sit with me in my throne, even as I also overcame, and am set down with my Father in his throne. He that hath an ear, let him hear what the Spirit saith unto the churches (Revelation 3:21–23).

A promise is made that we will sit with Him in His throne. If you open the door for Him, He will open one for you.

> After this I looked, and, behold, *a door was opened in heaven*: and the first voice which I heard *was* as it were of a trumpet talking with me; which said, Come up hither, and I will shew thee things which must be hereafter (Revelation 4:1, italics mine).

Imagine as you open up your door to Him, He answers by opening another door to you: a door to heaven. Praise God! Through His fellowship *a door* in heaven is opened to you. That door has to do with you. You have an inspired assignment - He gave authority to His servants and to every man His work-authored before the foundation of the earth. Jesus who is the author and the finisher of your faith was the one who wrote the plan. You gain access to the realm of the overcomers. You "porter" (carry) the image of heaven into the earth, you are a supernatural portal, *a door,* bringing with you the testimony of Jesus to super-impose on the earth what you see in heaven.

You hold a door open for Jesus, and then He opens a door for you...not a bad deal. Then you, having experienced being a porter, are able to show others how to transport heaven to earth.

Jesus operated in two realms simultaneously. Not only was He in a body walking the earth, but He also existed in heaven. This is true of us as well.

> If I have told you earthly things, and ye believe not, how shall ye believe, if I tell you *of* heavenly things? And no man hath ascended up to heaven, but he that came down from heaven, *even* the Son of man *which is in* heaven (John 3:11–13, italics mine).

Jesus was speaking to Nicodemus about two realms, one earthly and the other heavenly. He said that not only was He come down from heaven, but also was *in heaven* while simultaneously standing with Nicodemus. This is what a porter does; he stands in both realities simultaneously; porting what is needed from the kingdom, into the earthly realm. He closes and opens doors and gates between the two realities. The two realms exist simultaneously. Why not operate in both at one time? This is following Jesus example. His example is our model. He is the apostle and the high priest of our profession. We follow Him and have been given the mandate to walk even as He has walked.

> But whoso keepeth his word, in him verily is the love of God perfected: hereby know we that we are in him.He that saith he abideth in him ought himself also so to walk, even as he walked. (1 John 2:5–6).

John knew Jesus very well. John modeled himself after Jesus and he had his prayers answered. Listen to what he said about his own walk before God.

> And whatsoever we ask, we receive of him, because we keep his commandments, and do those things that are pleasing in his sight (1 John 3:22).

This is the assignment of the porter; having within himself both Jesus who is "the door" and a door (himself), opened up to heaven, granted him through relationship with Jesus. The porter has been given a watch at this door, he observes what is going on in the earthly realm, but monitors what he is seeing and hearing from the heavenly realm.

The porter adamantly insists that any difference between the two realms is a breach that can be repaired by bringing what is true in the heavenly places here to this earth. He brings the power of the kingdom into the breach, thereby repairing the breach between the two realities. You are a supernatural doorway or gateway between heaven and earth. On top of this, you exist in both places at once, just like Jesus does.

> But God, who is rich in mercy, for his great love wherewith he loved us, Even when we were dead in sins, hath quickened us together with Christ, (by grace ye are saved); And hath raised us up together, and made us sit together in heavenly places in Christ Jesus (Ephesians 2:4–6).

We are in heaven (in Him) and He is on earth in us. You are reading this book from a physical location, in the temporal realm of earth, yet simultaneously sitting with Christ in the eternal realm of heaven. Throughout the ages men have wondered how to bring heaven to earth: how to open up heaven on earth. How does His kingdom come?

When you first hear that His Kingdom must come through you, because it is in you…it is fantastic. How can you be expected to bring the kingdom? If the kingdom is within you, how can you release it from within? It must flow through you. When it does….

The Works of the Devil are Destroyed

> He that committeth sin is of the devil; for the devil sinneth from the beginning. For this purpose the Son of God was manifested, that he might destroy the works of the devil (1 John 3:8).

When Jesus rose from the dead he brought with Him the keys of hell and of death. Keys are the tool for locking and unlocking doors or gates. If a gate has been locked, you won't enter until you possess the key.

The Bible talks of a variety of doors and gates. **Gates of Death** Psalm 9:13; 107:18; Job 38:17; **The Grave**-Isaiah 38:10; **Of the rivers**-Nahum 2:6; **Of Hell**-Matthew 16:18; **Of the tabernacle**-1 Chronicles 9:19; **Of the daughter of Zion**-Psalm 9:14; **Of righteousness**-Psalm 118:19; **Of the righteous**-Proverbs 14:19; **Of the nobles**-Isaiah 13:2.

Gate of Your Enemies

> That in blessing I will bless thee, and in multiplying I will multiply thy seed as the stars of the heaven, and as the sand which is upon the sea shore; and thy seed shall possess *the gate of his enemies* (Genesis 22:17, italics mine).

Abraham was a half second away from offering Isaac as a sacrifice on Mt. Moriah when the angel of the Lord stayed his hand. It was clear to God that Abraham would not withhold his son Isaac, his only son, from God. God responded to his display of faith by blessing Abraham and promising to multiply his seed as the stars of heaven; and as the sand that is upon the sea shore. The second part of the blessing was **that his seed shall possess the gate of his enemies.**

> And if ye be Christ's, then are ye Abraham's seed, and heirs according to the promise (Galatians 3:29).

God withheld nothing from Abraham including the gate of his enemies, because Abraham withheld nothing from God. Because we are the seed of Abraham by being Christ's, we are heirs according to the promise. Through Christ we have become the seed of Abraham. The promise He gave to Abraham flows to you and me by faith in Christ Jesus.

Again in another place we see God's character in keeping His promise to Abraham:

> What shall we then say to these things? If God *be* for us, who *can be* against us? He that spared not his own Son, but delivered him up for us all, how shall he not with him also freely give us all things? (Romans 8:31–32).

And again:

> Therefore let no man glory in men. *For all things are yours*; Whether Paul, or Apollos, or Cephas, *or the world, or life, or death, or things present, or things to come; all are yours;* And ye are Christ's; and Christ *is* God's (1 Corinthians 3:21–23, italics mine).

He has withheld nothing, but look, it extends beyond things present or things to come. His promise is an **eternal one. You have been given the gate of all your enemies. All the gates have been given to you.**

THE KEYS OF THE KINGDOM

> When Jesus came into the coasts of Caesarea Philippi, he asked his disciples, saying, Whom do men say that I the Son of man am? (Matthew 16:13).
>
> And they said, Some *say that thou art* John the Baptist: some, Elias; and others, Jeremias, or one of the prophets. He saith unto them, But whom say ye that I am? And Simon Peter answered and said, Thou art the Christ, the Son of the living God. And Jesus answered and said unto him, Blessed art thou, Simon Barjona: for flesh and blood hath not revealed *it* unto thee, but my Father which is in heaven. And I say also unto thee, That thou art Peter, and upon this rock I will build my church; and the gates of hell shall not prevail against it. And I will give unto thee the *keys of the kingdom of heaven*: and whatsoever thou shalt bind on earth shall be bound in heaven: and whatsoever thou shalt loose on earth shall be loosed in heaven (Matthew 16:14–19, italics mine).

What was **the testimony** that released **the keys** of the kingdom of heaven to Peter? The answer that Peter gave when asked who Jesus was reveals the key, "thou art the Christ, the Son of the living God." Peter's **qualification** was a revelation of the "anointed one" the Christ. Jesus was revealed to him by the Father as the Christ, the Son! That is the revelation upon which the church is to be built and the revelation that releases *the Keys* of the kingdom of heaven. Peter was handed keys that locked doors and gates. When Peter locked them they were locked so tightly that all the power and authority of heaven stood watch over them; maintaining their seals. Any door he chose to open could not be shut…all of heaven agreed and **nothing** could shut it. **This is the authority given to you when you are holding those keys.** *Jesus wants to give you those keys.*

A porter with a set of keys, especially this set, would *overcome any lock* within gates or doors that **resist the kingdom from coming**. Also it would unlock gates, behind which, the lost have been held captive. The gates of hell "shall not prevail" against the church. *There is a key for every door.* The porter has the keys. The keys break open hell's resistance to the advancement of the kingdom. Jesus said He will build His church. Hell is no match for you when you are advancing the kingdom. The lost won't resist you when you have opened the gates of hell that have been holding them. When you open the door for the lost, they are excited to experience the regeneration and receive the power to become the sons of God.

The Master Key

> And it shall come to pass in that day, that I will call my servant Eliakim the son of Hilkiah: And I will clothe him with thy robe, and strengthen him with thy girdle, and I will commit thy government into his hand: and he shall be a father to the inhabitants of Jerusalem, and to the house of Judah. And the key of the house of David will I lay upon his shoulder; so he shall

open, and none shall shut; and he shall shut,
and none shall open (Isaiah 22:20–22).

Eliakim was given charge over the house of King David.
With this charge came a governmental key, the robe and girdle
of the Messiah. This endowment enabled him to administrate
the **king's house** with excellence. While it was a natural duty,
it had supernatural significance, because it was God's government. King David had been ordained by God and his kingdom
was part of the government of God. Therefore Eliakim was
given a supernatural key, the key of the house of David. *The
government was committed into his hand*.

Note that in the New Testament it says that, *you* are the
King's house. **As you steward the King's house, access to the
doors and gates are yours through God's government. You
are clothed in His robes, the girdle's strength belongs to you
and the government is committed into your hands; the government of the kingdom.**

Again in the Book of Revelation the one who is holy and
true and *in possession of the key of David* is instructing John to
write to the angel of the Church of Philadelphia.

And to the angel of the church in Philadelphia
write; These things saith he that is holy, he that
is true, he that hath the key of David, he that
openeth, and no man shutteth; and shutteth,
and no man openeth (Revelation 3:7).

When Jesus says something it is guaranteed. He has a key...
the key of David ... Jesus is the one who gives us the keys of the
kingdom. They will work for you as certainly as they worked
for Peter.

*There is an eternal purpose
for everything that God has done.*

> And to make *all men see* what *is the fellowship of the mystery*, which from the beginning of the world hath been hid in God, who created all things by Jesus Christ: *To the intent* that now unto the principalities and powers in heavenly *places* might be known by the church the manifold wisdom of God, According to *the eternal purpose* which he purposed in Christ Jesus our Lord (Ephesians 3:9–11, italics mine).

Part of the fellowship of the mystery is that the manifold wisdom of God would be evident to principalities and powers by what God has invested in the church. **The church is unstoppable**. It has been given the keys. Keys unlock doors and gates of resistance to all men who see the fellowship of the mystery that has been hidden in God. God is bringing His plan about in spite of all opposition, through us, His church. Imagine the confidence He has in the new creation.

I prophecy to you right now that you will permit yourself the freedom to grab those keys in your hand and release the kingdom. May God's grace expand your awareness of the power and authority He has placed in your spirit, because  you too have believed that He is the Christ, the Son of the living God. May you become one who opens kingdom doors and gates and brings the power of the age to come, everywhere it is needed. You will be one who lives simultaneously in heaven and on earth. You are the very gate of heaven and the house of God. Don't worry, you were designed by God, who cannot fail, to be a portal through which His kingdom flows. You have heaven's design.

For those of you that doubt that you have access to the keys, don't. They are available to all of us. You are the house of God and a gateway to heaven. You have an eternal purpose as a supernatural gateway within a supernatural house ... YOU.

The Controversial Key of Knowledge

> Woe unto you, lawyers! for ye have taken away
> the key of knowledge: ye entered not in your-
> selves, and them that were entering in ye hin-
> dered (Luke 11:52).

In the culture in which we live there are many politically correct precepts that carry increased pressure to conform to the evolving mindset of what is acceptable and what is allowed to be spoken for or against in public. Propaganda is released through messages in movies, talk shows, news media, etc. that seep into the minds of people.

At first, new information is foreign to the ear, but over time what seemed to be false or morally questionable becomes mainstream thinking. When the cultural doctrine has been accepted, laws change, and that which was once considered false or morally questionable, is protected and enforced.

By this time everyone knows that you can't say this but you can say that. You can do this but you can't do that. Within this new culture emerges a sort of self-policing where practically everyone speaks out against any violation of the new laws. They are like Pavlov's dogs when they hear the bell ring.

Jesus referred to this as the leaven of Herod:

> And he charged them, saying, Take heed,
> beware of the leaven of the Pharisees, and of the
> leaven of Herod (Mark 8:15).

The leaven of the Pharisees works the same way, except it occurs in the church. The leaven of Herod is societal engineering and the leaven of the Pharisees is religious engineering. Both are dangerous to us and cause us to trust the government and Christian leaders more than God Himself.

There are many things said by Christians that are patently false that do not hold up against scriptural scrutiny, yet they are taught as if they were "the truth."

If I were to say " I can raise the dead" or "I can heal the sick" some Christians, like Pavlov's dogs, would immediately begin to correct me according to the way they see things and insist that, "nobody raises the dead or heals the sick but God!" Why is this? I think it is because the teachers and preachers within the church have expressed and preached such notions until the leaven of the Pharisees has leavened much of the body of Christ. **Ye entered not in yourselves, and *them that were entering in ye hindered*** (Luke 11:52). The only way to defeat such leaven is to grab the key of knowledge and not let go. This means you must live by what God says. If you simply accept what you are taught by others as truth, not investigating the Bible for yourself, you are not wise. You must know what God has said. When God's word conflicts with what men say; always choose what God says, and reject what is said by men, regardless of whom that man is (anyone can be effected by leaven, that's why Jesus warned his disciples). Learn to get your own revelation from God. Learn to study for yourself what God says about everything. You must eat from the hand of God, not the hand of man.

But can I raise the dead or heal the sick? I would say to you "yes I can. I can prove it!"

Bring me dead bodies and infirmed people and I will do exactly what Jesus said I would be able to do.

To all the scoffers who get upset when I do what Jesus has empowered me to do I say "too bad for you, but your unbelief is not going to keep me out of the kingdom because the kingdom is the King's domain and Jesus is my King." I do not follow anyone who is not truly following Him, the words of a stranger I will not follow. If the words of men do not line up with God's words, then they are strange words. As one of his sheep, I will follow him. **This is what is meant by believing on Him as the scripture has said.**

> He that believeth on me, as the scripture hath said, out of his belly shall flow rivers of living water (John 7:38).

> Verily, verily, I say unto you, He that believeth on me, the works that I do shall he do also; and greater works than these shall he do; because I go unto my Father (John 14:12).

This key of knowledge and the message within it frees me to believe what God said instead of what any man says. This key of knowledge unlocks the freedom I need to operate as a son of God, empowered as an ambassador of Christ to do works in His Name.

The religious leaven creates a barrier to those who would enter the kingdom and truly work the works of God. "Ye entered not in yourselves, and them that were entering in ye hindered" (Luke 11:52).

Because the leaven has moved throughout the church, the knee jerk reaction is to warn the poor confused brother who is daring to believe God and is raising the dead and healing the sick that he must be in error because he is doing something uncommon or unheard of. However, having dealt with such unbelief many times, that man keeps on working the works of God because he refuses to allow those corrupted by the leaven to effect his own believing.

Jesus instructed us to avoid the constraints of leaven. It is also what Jesus modeled for us during His earthly ministry. Jesus was always challenged by the religious establishment about where He got His authority to perform miracles and His teaching. He consistently called them on their hypocrisy and rebuked them and we can do the same. Jesus warned his disciples they too would suffer persecution. Don't be surprised when it happens to you; keep following Jesus.

MY DISCOVERY AND ACCEPTANCE OF THE MINISTRY OF THE PORTER

Guard your hearts with all diligence against this leaven.

During a conference, I was listening to a speaker who taught on the scripture in Psalm 24.

> Lift up your heads, O ye gates; and be ye lift up, ye everlasting doors; and the King of glory shall come in. Who is this King of glory? The LORD strong and mighty, the LORD mighty in battle. Lift up your heads, O ye gates; even lift them up, ye everlasting doors; and the King of glory shall come in (Psalm 24:7–9).

Once I discovered that I was both a gate and a door, I began to speak openly amongst my friends about this, sharing what I understood. One day while sharing a meal at a restaurant with a friend of mine, Donna Layden, I told her about how I minister. And for the first time these words came out of my mouth, "When I lead a person **to the door of healing**, I begin by taking them through the scriptures. Then when they understand enough I will pray for them and they are healed."

I thought it very curious that I would use such wording as **"the door of healing."** Yet while thinking about it further it made sense. By much experience, I have always believed that if I can elevate the level of a person's faith to the point they can believe, I can heal them. I have countless hours with hundreds of people where I took the time to instruct them to the point where they believed that they would be healed when we prayed. Only God knows how many.

Then one day I heard the internal voice of God say to me, "You are my porter." I thought to myself, "what do You mean by that?" That day He opened my understanding of a specific role presented by Jesus concerning His sheepfold and those positioned to keep watch and open doors to Him. The more I investigated this the clearer the picture became. I had never heard this revelation in the more than 23 years of walking with God. But now, what I had been doing in ministry began to make perfect sense to me. I had already been acting in this role of a porter and didn't even know that I was operating in is a Biblical mandate. Through following Christ, doing what I believed He was leading me to do, I intuitively had opened doors and gates for others.

I thought of how this ministry might be useful. When I met people who needed doors opened to them for a job, I prayed as a porter and declared what I saw in the mind of Christ in my capacity as a porter. From the position of a porter I would prophetically open a door for them to be hired. Each time I have done this they knew something just happened in the spirit realm that made a way for them to find a job. I thought that was pretty cool; being able to open doors for others.

Just the other day, my friend Terry Markovich and I were ministering to a well-known brother of ours, who for the last 23 years, was unable to sleep for more than 20 minutes at a time. He was being tormented by reasonings, condemnation and self doubts. For the last several decades he has served Christ faithfully in his city.

On the first day, after praying for him, he slept for five hours but during the last hour he was tormented in his dreams. He remembered that he was to pray in tongues to defeat the voices so he prayed for a while. He got sleepy and went to sleep for a couple more hours. The next day we met again. While in prayer the Lord took us to the place where the torment had entered his life. When he understood what had happened to open this door of torment we were able to break the power of those voices. After about an hour of prayer I took a key and prophetically locked the door that had been opened so many years ago. Now this brother sleeps through the night and understands his freedom. He is totally set free. The voices are gone. That is the power that we have as porters. We can shut doors so tightly that nothing can ever open them again. Heaven has sealed them by our intentional diligence to not only understand the authority that we have, but also to use it.

Long ago, having a desire to see heaven on earth, my heart opened the supernatural gateway between heaven and earth. Passion and a relentless pursuit to see His kingdom manifested kept the door opened by faith. In ever increasing ways the power of the kingdom continued to flow through this channel. What I didn't realize was that I am that channel. I am the access point and doorway into the supernatural...and so are you!

> The secret things belong unto the LORD our God: but those things which are revealed belong unto us and to our children forever, that we may do all the words of this law (Deuteronomy 29:29).

Things *secret* belong to the Lord, but when they are revealed, they belong to us and to our children forever...they help us to be doers of the Word. I don't know about you, but such revelations mean a lot to me. They are more valuable than rubies. I latch onto them with all my heart and immediately include them in my meditations and activate them because I have discovered the potential of them to set many free. The greatest part of all is that once understood, these secrets belong to me and my children forever. How cool is that?

BECOME LIKE A LITTLE CHILD

Children Imagine. Unfettered imagination easily accepts and rejoices in being able to participate in great adventures. Children are hungry to experience and to explore. Children excite easily. If you tell them good news, especially if it concerns them, they are instantly open to it and eager to see it come to pass. They seem able to rise to whatever bar you set for them and look to parents for guidance.

My daughter is a great example. When she was an infant, I rocked her to sleep in a rocking chair. While putting her to sleep I always sang worship songs to her. And I prophesied over her future during these priceless moments. I would say that she "eschewed evil and loved righteousness, therefore God, her God gave her the oil of joy above her companions." I also prophesied that "she grow waxing strong in the Spirit and increase in favor with both God and man." I prophesied many things over her life, but my favorite was that "she always did that which was right in the sight of God."

When my daughter was a little girl I used to take her to the park during my lunch break from work. Kids looking for someone to play with often approached her. She played with them for a while and eventually she would ask them a question "Do you know Jesus?" When they answered no, she yelled across the playground to me, "Hey Dad over here!! This girl doesn't know Jesus." I had to be ready at all times to introduce children to Jesus, because my daughter kept me busy.

It is no wonder to me that she is successful at everything she does and that she despises evil.

My daughter used to ask me to tell her stories about when I was the same age as she. She loves stories. Our bedtime stories were out of the Bible and out of our family history.

One night I said to her, "I have a family secret I would like to share with you. All Hanks are geniuses! Our whole family is filled with people who are very intelligent."

"Really Daddy?" she inquired, "Tell me stories about this."

I went through a few stories to lend credibility to such a bold declaration. Then I said to her, "so you see my daughter, you are an extremely wise and smart person, you might as well get used to it; you will be very successful and will rise right to the top in everything you put your hand to."

"Really Daddy?" she replied.

I said, "absolutely; you can count on it!"

She received that night a crucial foundation for her concept of self and has totally lived up to these prophetic words. The prophetic words led to prophetic acts of fulfillment. She became the words. She lived the words, she achieved the words.

You are no different than she is. You were created in the likeness of God and as you escape the corruptions that are in the world through lust, you partake of His divine nature. You are a genius. A religious spirit will try to keep everyone believing they are nothing and God is everything…this is not true. He has raised you up together with Christ and made you to sit together with Him in heavenly places. You are amazing!

Harsh and critical words can rob children of their future by wounding them in their deepest parts. But God will heal you if you have suffered evil prophecies from others that have bound you into negative self-concepts. Jesus has come to set you free from these restrictive curses, so that your childlike wonder returns, and as He whispers to you how wonderful you are, your healing will come. Whatever He touches lives! Be restored to the truth of who you are. You are a gateway of heaven within the house of God! Praise the Lord!

I prophesy right now that you will wax strong in the spirit, increasing in favor with both God and man. You will live out the benefits of your prophetic birthright in Christ. You will bring much needed love and healing to those around you and you will do things that currently seem beyond your reach that will amaze you and thrill you. God has breathed upon you; His plans for you will come to pass. You will stand in the victory your heart has longed for. The Holy Spirit will make this prophetic word real to you as you allow God to establish your prophetic identity in Him. You are beautiful. You are a masterpiece crafted by the master of assemblies. He will heal you. You will be very content and happy as a porter for the King and His kingdom, in the Glorious name of Jesus, our Messiah. AMEN! Say "I agree!"

8

WHO POURED WATER ON THE PROPHET?

For Moses truly said unto the fathers, A prophet shall the Lord your God raise up unto you of your brethren, like unto me; him shall ye hear in all things whatsoever he shall say unto you. And it shall come to pass, that every soul, which will not hear that prophet, shall be destroyed from among the people. Yea, and all the prophets from Samuel and those that follow after, as many as have spoken, have likewise foretold of these days. Ye are the children of the prophets, and of the covenant which God made with our fathers, saying unto Abraham, And in thy seed shall all the kindreds of the earth be blessed. Unto you first God, having raised up his Son Jesus, sent him to bless you, in turning away every one of you from his iniquities (Acts 3:21–26).

Moses spoke of Christ as did all the prophets. Christ came to bless all of us and to turn every one of us from our iniquities. What is not well known is the mystery hidden in plain sight within verse 25 "Ye are the children of the prophets."

The seemingly obvious meaning to the natural mind is that the audience was Jewish; the natural descendants through genealogy. The *promise to Abraham is that the blessing includes "ALL kindreds of the earth" verse 25. Christ was raised* up to turn away "every one of you" from your iniquities. On second look it becomes even more obvious that He is talking to everyone on the entire planet; this includes you.

John chapter eight opens with the woman caught in the act of adultery.

> And the scribes and Pharisees brought unto him a woman taken in adultery; and when they had set her in the midst, They say unto him, Master, this woman was taken in adultery, in the very act. Now Moses in the law commanded us, that such should be stoned: but what sayest thou? This they said, tempting him, that they might have to accuse him. But Jesus stooped down, and with *his* finger wrote on the ground, *as though he heard them not.* So when they continued asking him, he lifted up himself, and said unto them, He that is without sin among you, let him first cast a stone at her. And again he stooped down, and wrote on the ground. And they which heard *it, being convicted by their own conscience*, went out one by one, beginning at the eldest, even unto the last: and Jesus was left alone, and the woman standing in the midst. When Jesus had lifted up himself, and saw none but the woman, he said unto her, Woman, where are those thine accusers? hath no man condemned thee? She said, No man, Lord. And

> Jesus said unto her, Neither do I condemn thee:
> go, and sin no more (John 8:3–11, italics mine).

Usually when you hear a sermon on this incident it is given in the context of the forgiveness of God. Our attention is drawn to the way in which Jesus handled the situation, who looked at the woman with compassion, and to the crowd who want to stone the woman. The wisdom of God is displayed when Jesus said that the first stone be cast by the one in the group without sin; **Jesus was the only one qualified to hit her with a rock.** However, He wanted what God has always wanted, so He rescued her with wisdom instead.

As the story unfolds each person holding a rock was convicted by his conscience and walked away leaving the woman alone with Jesus. When I heard this story taught, the message usually ended there, so I just assumed that everybody left the scene.

But I was wrong, the ones incited to stone the woman had left, but those who had incited the mob and staged the whole event stayed. Jesus had robbed them of their evil expectations. They remained and saw Jesus forgive the woman and heard what He said right after that.

The ones who really had murder in their hearts were these scribes and Pharisees. They wanted to get rid of Jesus.

Now Jesus, after speaking to those gathered to kill the woman, now addressed the real killers.

> Then spake Jesus again unto them, saying, I am the light of the world: he that followeth me shall not walk in darkness, but shall have the light of life. The Pharisees therefore said unto him, Thou bearest record of thyself; thy record is not true. Jesus answered and said unto them, Though I bear record of myself, yet my record is true: for I know whence I came, and whither

I go; but ye cannot tell whence I come, and whither I go. Ye judge after the flesh; I judge no man.

And yet if I judge, my judgment is true: for I am not alone, but I and the Father that sent me.

It is also written in your law, that the testimony of two men is true. I am one that bear witness of myself, and the Father that sent me beareth witness of me. Then said they unto him, Where is thy Father? Jesus answered, Ye neither know me, nor my Father: if ye had known me, ye should have known my Father also. These words spake Jesus in the treasury, as he taught in the temple: and no man laid hands on him; for his hour was not yet come. Then said Jesus again unto them, I go my way, and ye shall seek me, and shall die in your sins: whither I go, ye cannot come. Then said the Jews, Will he kill himself? because he saith, Whither I go, ye cannot come. And he said unto them, Ye are from beneath; I am from above: ye are of this world; I am not of this world (John 8:11–23).

Jesus tells the religious leaders that He is from above but they are from beneath. He was sent from His Father (God) and the religious leaders are of their father the devil. If they fail to believe that He is the one sent from God that they would die in their sins.

Jesus goes on:

Then said Jesus to those Jews which believed on him, If ye continue in my word, then are ye my disciples indeed; And ye shall know the

> truth, and the truth shall make you free. They
> answered him, We be Abraham's seed, and were
> never in bondage to any man: how sayest thou,
> Ye shall be made free? Jesus answered them,
> Verily, verily, I say unto you, Whosoever com-
> mitteth sin is the servant of sin. And the servant
> abideth not in the house forever: but the Son
> abideth ever (John 8:31–35).

They may have been descendants of Abraham through genealogy but without Christ they were the children of Satan. Christ was the seed of Abraham which would become the genetic blueprint of everyone born from the dead. **In Christ alone are we Abraham's seed and heirs according to the promise.**

Jesus identified them as servants of sin, and therefore children of the devil because His words found no place in them.

> For Moses truly said unto the fathers, a prophet
> shall the Lord your God raise up unto you of
> your brethren, like unto me; him shall ye hear
> in all things whatsoever he shall say unto you
> (Acts 3:22).

Jesus was "that prophet" who was speaking, but His words were not heeded, they found no place in the Pharisees and scribes. Their fate was sealed, they had a different father. Their father was a murderer from the beginning.

But thank God, those who have believed that Jesus is the one who was the blessing of Abraham, who turns every one of us away from our iniquities, have a new father now. Our Father is God. We received a new nature. Our nature is a divine nature which comes to us because we have been born again out of the incorruptible seed of the word of God. His words have found a home in us.

> Ye are the children of the prophets, and of the covenant which God made with our fathers, saying unto Abraham, And in thy seed shall all the kindreds of the earth be blessed (Acts 3:25).

If through Christ, You have become a child of the prophets, you are also a prophet. Your DNA in Christ is prophetic DNA. You are prophetic because of the new birth in Christ. You are a child of the prophets and a child of every promise made to Abraham in Christ Jesus. You are a child of promise and a prophetic child.

WHAT IS PROPHESY?

> But he that prophesieth speaketh unto men to edification, and exhortation, and comfort. He that speaketh in an unknown tongue edifieth himself; but he that prophesieth edifieth the church (1 Corinthians 14:3–4).

To prophesy is to speak edification, exhortation and comfort to others. In Christ, as part of the make-up of our new nature, we now understand the prophetic reality of the new creation. We have all become prophetic by the divine nature we have received.

Prophesy is sometimes cloaked in mystery. When you don't know what it is or how you instinctively operate in prophetic ways, you fail to realize your ministry within the body of Christ.

Edifying the Church

He that prophesies edifies the church.

How is it then, brethren? when ye come together, every one of you hath a psalm, hath a doctrine, hath a tongue, hath a revelation, hath an interpretation. *Let all things be done unto edifying* (1 Corinthians 14:26, italics mine).

For *ye may all prophesy* one by one, *that all may learn*, and *all may be comforted* (1 Corinthians 14:31, italics mine).

Anytime you speak to another in edification, exhortation, or comfort, you have utilized the prophetic nature you were given in Christ. Any time you have comforted others with the same comfort God has comforted you, you have performed a prophetic act. Anytime you have used the scriptures to point someone towards freedom in Christ, you have performed a prophetic act. Anytime, through the scriptures you have built another up (edify), you have performed a prophetic act. **You and I do this out of a desire to edify one another in love**. This is both intuitive and instinctual because of the prophetic nature of the inward man. Many of you are realizing that according to Paul's definition of prophecy (speaking unto men in edification, exhortation and comfort), you have been engaged in prophecy but did not know it. Now that you understand that you have been operating this way for some time, you see that you are prophetic. You have comforted others using the truth of God's word. You have helped others out of a jam through revelation that God has given you. You are a child of the prophets.

The Spirit is willing but the flesh is weak. It is the spirit of man which is the prophetic child of the prophets. The inward man is so very willing to operate in the way that he was designed by God to operate.

Understanding your prophetic nature is the key to waking up to your personal calling to edify the church; to speak unto men in edification, exhortation and comfort.

I began to operate in my prophetic calling shortly after being filled with the Holy Ghost. Instinctively I began to do this. No one told me to, I just had a knowing that what I was hearing and receiving in the word would be of benefit to others, so I began to share those things that I was learning. Isn't it only natural to want to share good news?

When people would thank me for sharing truth with them, I realized that they were being helped or edified. Often the very thing proceeding out of my mouth was exactly what they needed at the time. The other reality is that when you speak the words of Christ, they are spirit and they are life. I was speaking His word. Burdens would come off others. But they also came off of me. I would be edified in the same way that those hearing would be edified. I often found that I would be speaking to myself at the same time. This was interesting to me. The boomerang effect of edification was very healing to me also.

This reality was puzzling to me.

Why was it that *out of my mouth came words* that helped others? Why was it happening? Was there something special about me? Yes there was. I had become a new creation with a prophetic nature. I am a child of the prophets. And so are you.

This kept happening and people would label me according to their *perception* depending on how I had helped them; they would label me according to what was being received by them in the moment. Some would call me a pastor, others an evangelist. As these prophetic acts kept coming out from me, new labels emerged. I was called a prophet, a teacher, an apostle. I suppose that is because Jesus was each of these, the prophetic acts may have varied in what they accomplished person to person, but through the lens I was viewed, the labels changed according to what part of my new nature had been experienced.

When I reminded someone of the apostle Paul, they would label me as an apostle. Isn't this interesting? When a person saw the prophetic part of my new nature, they would call it out. They would call me a prophet. When they saw the evangelistic part of my new nature, they would say something. When they saw the apostolic part of my new nature they would mention it or just call me an apostle. I found this very interesting. Prophetically, all of these labels found a home in me.

When I went to Nigeria for the first time, I noticed that the people freely called one another after the gifts given to men.

> And he gave some, apostles; and some, prophets; and some, evangelists; and some, pastors and teachers (Ephesians 4:11).

You would hear them call a brother an apostle, a pastor or an evangelist. This was quite common. They would call one another "Man of God" or "Woman of God." I was blessed that in their land they spoke of God freely and without shame; it did not matter to them who was listening. They live authentically and unashamedly. I was blessed by this. I was proud to be among them, to call them my brothers and sisters, for truly they are. It was strange to my ears at first, having heard so many voices in North America frown on anyone claiming to be an "apostle."

The same people, in North America, have no problem with a man calling himself a pastor or a teacher, but somehow you deserve a stern rebuke if you say you are an apostle or a prophet. It is foolish to accept one of the gifts without treating the others with equal acceptance. The Nigerians have no problem at all receiving you. In fact they rejoice in you, knowing that we all have a supply of the spirit of Jesus Christ, and that every part of his body gives life to the joints to which they are attached. Now it is very easy for me to feel joy when a Nigerian addresses me as an apostle.

Perhaps they see a mystery that North Americans have been taught to reject. It is interesting to me to go to other nations that see things differently because they don't have the same mindset.

I have now come to realize that the new nature is a five-fold nature. Why else would it require all five offices to perfect the saints? The apostle is needed to perfect the apostolic part of the new nature; the prophet is required to perfect the prophetic part; the pastor to perfect the pastoral part; the evangelist to perfect the evangelistic part and the teacher to perfect the teaching part.

ELIJAH HAD A SCHOOL OF THE PROPHETS.

And the sons of the prophets said unto Elisha, Behold now, the place where we dwell with thee is too strait for us. Let us go, we pray thee, unto Jordan, and take thence every man a beam, and let us make us a place there, where we may dwell. And he answered, Go ye. And one said, Be content, I pray thee, and go with thy servants. And he answered, I will go. So he went with them. And when they came to Jordan, they cut down wood. But as one was felling a beam, the axe head fell into the water: and he cried, and said, Alas, master! for it was borrowed. And the man of God said, Where fell it? And he shewed him the place. And he cut down a stick, and cast it in thither; and the iron did swim. Therefore said he, Take it up to thee. And he put out his hand, and took it (2 Kings 6:1–7).

It is interesting that God used the same words in 2 Kings 6 and in Acts 3:25 in reference to the sons of the prophets. These men who were students of Elisha were described as sons of the prophets. Notice what Elisha said to Elijah when he saw the chariot?

> And it came to pass, as they still went on, and talked, that, behold, there appeared a chariot of fire, and horses of fire, and parted them both asunder; and Elijah went up by a whirlwind into heaven. And Elisha saw it, and he cried, *My father, my father*, the chariot of Israel, and the horsemen thereof. And he saw him no more: and he took hold of his own clothes, and rent them in two pieces (2 Kings 2:11–12, italics mine).

He called Elijah father. When Elijah had thrown his mantle upon him years before he assumed the role of his son. He called him father until the day that he was taken up in the chariot. This reality and the spirit of it carried right over into the early church. When I desire to be fathered by those who come before me in the Lord, I take the position of son. "Ye are the sons of the Prophets."

In Nigeria you will notice this is also carried on today. I was with Pastor Gabriel and he introduced me to a couple of young women. He said "this is my daughter." In my North American world we introduce our natural children as daughters or sons. He kept introducing me to others who he referred to as sons and daughters. Not understanding their traditions I assumed that he was a very busy man.

Although he has seven or eight children of his own he has many hundreds of spiritual children who call him daddy. These are mostly orphans that he has personally put through school or college. He has taken responsibility for them and has provided for them. Wow. He has done a lot and they all revere him. If he tells one of them to take a week off from school and help him in the ministry, they will drop everything they are doing, and without a trace of complaining they will obey him without question. Wow. When you realize that he is equally committed to their success you realize the respect goes both ways. On my third trip to Nigeria I got to minister to some young people and a few of them called me daddy. I tell you that meant a lot to me. I felt special to have a position of such honor in the heart of a young man or woman; to be held in such a high regard due to my work for the Lord. I now understand the relationship between Elijah and Elisha and between Elisha and his students. They were raising sons. And so am I.

> He that delicately bringeth up his servant from
> a child shall have him become *his* son at the
> length (Proverbs 29:21).

This care for others is highly valued in Nigeria. We could learn a lot from them, I know I have.

> But as one was felling a beam, the axe head fell
> into the water: and he cried, and said, Alas,
> master! for it was borrowed. And the man of
> God said, Where fell it? And he shewed him the
> place. And he cut down a stick, and cast it in
> thither; and the iron did swim. Therefore said
> he, Take it up to thee. And he put out his hand,
> and took it (2 Kings 6:5–7).

His axe head flew off when he was cutting wood and was lost in the river. He was troubled because it was a borrowed axe. So the master, father Elisha asked him where it fell?

Maybe you were hewing for the Lord at one point. Your axe head might have flew off into the river. The circumstances of life came along, a divorce, or a death, or you became offended. Any number of events might have happened to you. When it did, you lost something. You cannot continue until you get it back. You may feel useless, or that it is too late for you, or that you are too old and your fruitful season cannot be retrieved.

What is your axe head? When did you last know you were effective? Jesus wants to go with you; you can talk to Him about it. He cares about you. You can show Him where your life and or ministry went into the river and at the exact place it happened. He is going back there with you today. He will throw a stick in the river and your axe head will come back into your hand; you will become effective again. Praise the Lord! I prophesy that today is your day. You have been lying in the ashes of yesterday, but today you will arise out of that long dark valley and be stronger than you were before in the mighty name of Jesus! Your Father is an expert at bringing things back to you. You are a child of the prophets and of the covenant that God made with Abraham.

> And he gave some, apostles; and some, prophets; and some, evangelists; and some, pastors and teachers; For the perfecting of the saints, for the work of the ministry, for the edifying of the body of Christ: Till we all come in the unity of the faith, and of the knowledge of the Son of God, unto a perfect man, unto the measure of the stature of the fulness of Christ: That we henceforth be no more children, tossed to and fro, and carried about with every wind of doctrine, by the sleight of men, and cunning craftiness, whereby they lie in wait to deceive (Ephesians 4:11–14).

My desire to become perfected caused me to seek out those called to the office of a prophet so I could learn and come into a working understanding of my prophetic nature. As I was trained and activated in my prophetic DNA, I began to speak unto men in edification, exhortation and comfort. Often prophesy was activated automatically just by being in the company of a prophet.

> After that thou shalt come to the hill of God, where *is* the garrison of the Philistines: and it shall come to pass, when thou art come thither to the city, that thou shalt meet a company of prophets coming down from the high place with a psaltery, and a tabret, and a pipe, and a harp, before them; and they shall prophesy: And the Spirit of the LORD will come upon thee, and thou shalt prophesy with them, *and shalt be turned into another man* (1 Samuel 10:5–6, italics mine).

I have had such encounters. One day I had nothing, the next day I was another man. Coming into the company of one called to the office of a prophet will change you. It changed me, I began to prophesy; the same Spirit that was upon the prophet activated the prophetic part of my new nature.

After that I grew and through the unction of prophesy I continue to edify the church. One day I may be chosen to stand in the office of a prophet. I will do that if the Lord desires and chooses me, but until then I am glad to prophesy and buildup or edify those connected to me through the Lord.

I have placed myself under those who were placed into the office of a teacher. I received from them and was able to teach others also.

> And the things that thou hast heard of me among many witnesses, the same commit thou to faithful men, who shall be able to teach others also (2 Timothy 2:2).

> For when for the time ye ought to be teachers,
> ye have need that one teach you again which be
> the first principles of the oracles of God; and
> are become such as have need of milk, and not
> of strong meat (Hebrews 5:12).

Interesting…Paul believed that there came a time when all should be able to *teach*. He told Timothy to commit the things he had learned to faithful men who would be able to *teach* others also. The instruction needs to continue within every generation. How else would it continue without us? If not us, then who?

When these parts of your inner man are perfected you are:

1. Discerning and stable; not falling for unfounded doctrines

2. Cannot be fooled by craftiness of men.

3. Grown up…no longer children in understanding.

4. You remind everyone who sees you of Jesus. You have grown up into Him that is the head.

> That we henceforth be no more children, tossed
> to and fro, and carried about with every wind of
> doctrine, by the sleight of men, and cunning
> craftiness, whereby they lie in wait to deceive
> (Ephesians 4:14).

I still see immaturity in myself, but I also notice Christ in me, the hope of Glory, shining like the brightness of the sun as I continue to grow and do whatever is needed. Others don't understand me, but I don't care, I was not called by those who don't believe in me, but I was called by the One who does. He has called you too. Let Him define you as you study His word.

Often, right in front of me, is another opportunity to minister out of my inward man, my new nature. Out of the treasure placed in this earthen vessel, the power of the Highest changes things and people, because I have been born from above, and have been made partaker of His divine nature. I am my Father's son.

I hope this book causes you to see how marvelously God has designed you. You were created for His glory. His glory has risen upon you. Rather than pretending you are nothing and unworthy, why don't you just arise and shine, radiating the glory He has placed in the jar of clay you call your body. He calls it His house. He likes living in you. He likes fellowshipping with you. He wants to empower you. He wishes for all His children to come into their full inheritance. Don't allow anyone to steal your crown.

Step into your full inheritance. Don't allow the cunning craftiness of men to deceive you. Awaken from your sleep and Christ will give you light. Give a glass of cold water to the prophet sitting next to you.

God has used me to wake up a few prophets. I have known people called by God to be prophets but were not awaken to their calling. They sat passively in pews of churches for years, asleep to the calling. Until someone (me) came along and began to call out the prophet.

What I mean is this. I would notice the grace upon them. I didn't know what it was at the time, but through spending time with a person you see deeper into them. You begin to prophesy to them. Speaking unto them in edification, exhortation and comfort. You build them up. As they are transformed through the connection, loved into wholeness, and plugged into heaven's wall socket, you start noticing how they operate by the spirit. You see that the predominant manifestation is that of a prophet and like others they encounter, you start calling them a prophet. Somehow they begin to see in themselves what others are already noticing. Selah.

Of course before they were lullabied to sleep sitting in the church, they were actually exhibiting signs of the calling, but had been discouraged and lost hope that what they saw was

more than just a coincidence. But speaking unto them in edification, exhortation and comfort, was the equivalent of someone
pouring cold water upon one who was in a deep sleep. All of a
sudden they are operating once again as God destined them to
operate, simply because God breathed upon him through the
love of another one of his children.

What an honor it is to discover the vessels discarded and
bruised, through organized religion and unbelief, and walk
beside them until they understand who they are and recon-
nected to their purpose. I can't think of a higher honor than
this. These beloved saints are all around us all the time; kings
that do not know how to wear royal garments or how to scatter
the wicked with just a glance.

Many of us have been dragged before Jesus by the sons of
Satan. They reject us, malign us and cast us down. But God is
ready to declare to us that no man accuses us before Him. He
has come to pick us up. He has come to show us our marvelous
inheritance in Him, elevating us with Him to be seated in the
place of rest at the right hand of the father.

From this heavenly position He will show you the mysteries of the kingdom and release you into the harvest as an
instrument crafted in the fire; a sharp threshing instrument,
one that has sharp teeth. You are a royal priesthood and a Holy
Nation. Never allow any man to define you otherwise. They are
liars; but God is true. When we allow His love to take hold of
our hearts, we can be a great blessing to those around us. We
can lead many back onto the path.

When we see each other according to the flesh we easily miss
it. But when we know each other according to the Spirit we just
might be able to prophesy out of the mind of Christ, lifting them
up, building them up and walking with them in the light as Jesus
is in the light, having fellowship one with another, all the while
the precious blood of Jesus is cleansing us from sin.

Isn't it marvelous working with the Lord? He takes loving
care of each of us and has said that the predominant sign that
we are believers is the love that we have one for another. Isn't

it a blessing to see someone come up higher because you cared enough to take the time? Isn't it great when you see someone healed through love and caring, as well as through the signs miracles and wonders of our God available to us in the name of Jesus.

His name is as an ointment poured forth. His name carries all authority in heaven and on the earth. Wouldn't it be wonderful if everyone knew how to work with Him in this way? You will learn how. You can do it.

That is where you are special, unique. Not everyone has gone through what you have been through. Your unique experience qualifies you to minister as only you can. You are able to give hope to others who are experiencing the same things you went through. You can tell them about what happened to you and how God helped you. You'll be able to encourage them to endure what's upon them, never giving up hope, because they are comforted with the same comfort wherewith God has comforted you. These are prophetic acts. They lift us higher. They build us up.

You are every bit as capable of helping others, as anyone else. You have a new nature. You have the life of God in you: you are a child of the prophets and a child of the covenant, because of what Jesus did on the cross.

We are all called to do something. To pick up your brother or sister who has been knocked down and falsely accused at the feet of Jesus. Help them as Jesus did the woman caught in the act of adultery, who needed someone to point the way out of her darkness and speak words of life. Stand up for those who have been appointed unto death. Intercept their path as they are stumbling in the dark on their way to hell without a savior. Turn them around with the love of God; bring them through the door into the sheepfold. Become a roadblock on the way to hell. Don't let anyone get passed you, instead help them.

Love one another.

9

GIVING WITNESS
TO HIS RESURRECTION

And with great power gave the apostles witness of the resurrection of the Lord Jesus: and great grace was upon them all (Acts 4:33).

Yesterday I was going to western union to send money to a friend. As I drove up to the business I noticed a sign in the window informing customers that the store was closed for the remainder of the day due to a computer failure. The ladies that ran the store were closing up. I asked them where I might find another outlet from which to send the money. After they told me where to go I got back in my car to drive away. As I pulled out of the parking lot I looked around the corner of the building and these two ladies were carrying cardboard to deposit in the dumpsters around back. I noticed that one of the ladies was walking with a cane. I turned around and drove up beside them. I rolled the window down and said to the lady with the cane, "I noticed that you walk with a cane; how long have you done so?" "Four years," she replied. I said, "what a coincidence.

Just yesterday I prayed for a man who took a fall from a lad-
der, shattered his ankle in several places, and has been using
a cane since. He is unable to walk but rather shuffles his feet
in tiny steps and moving very slowly. When we prayed he was
instantly healed by the power of God and no longer needs the
cane to walk. I wonder if you would like me to pray for you so
you don't have to walk with a cane anymore?" "Yes I would,"
she said. I told her that I would pull over and pray for her. She
wanted to take her trash to dumpster and said she'd be right
back. I waited a few minutes then peeked around the corner
only to see that the two ladies were enjoying a cigarette break
by the dumpster. When they saw me waiting they cut it short
and started back. As they approached me they were engaged in
what seemed to be an intense conversation. I waited for them
and readied my Bible to the 5th chapter of James.

When they reached me the friend of the lady who needed
healing asked me if I would allow her to help pray for her
friend because she believed in healing and that they had been
talking about healing at the dumpster. I welcomed her warmly
to join us.

I learned that Justine had been a figure skater in her early
years and had fallen on her right hip several times injuring it.
After all these injuries arthritis had set into the hip joint. It
caused continuous pain in her hip making it impossible for her
to walk without the use of the cane for the last four years.

I pulled out a bottle of scented anointing oil; the fragrance
was frankincense and myrrh. I asked if they remembered the
Christmas story of the birth of Jesus and of the wise men who
followed the star from the east to look for the new king that
should be born. "As you may remember," I said, "they brought
gifts for little baby Jesus. These gifts were very valuable – gold,
frankincense and myrrh. Well this oil combines the two fragrances. You are in for a treat because you will get to smell
what Jesus smelled when He was just a baby and not only
that you will be healed too." The ladies were excited that they

remembered this Biblical account and anticipated the marvelous promise that Justine would walk without a cane.

> Is any sick among you? let him call for the elders of the church; and let them pray over him, anointing him with oil in the name of the Lord: And the prayer of faith shall save the sick, and the Lord shall raise him up; and if he have committed sins, they shall be forgiven him (James 5:14).

I quoted this scripture to them and explained the purpose of the oil and its use in praying the prayer of faith. "This is why I have the oil. It is a sign that I believe and have faith that you will be healed. As an added bonus any sins that you have committed will be forgiven you as we pray, so not only will you be healed, but you start fresh with a clean slate before God."

This was appealing to Justine and we were all very excited with anticipation.

It says in the book of Acts that **with great power gave the apostles witness of the resurrection of the Lord Jesus: and great grace was upon them all (Acts 4:33).**

I also said, "Jesus died on the cross for the sins of the whole world, was buried and laid in the grave for three days, but after the third day He was raised from the dead. This is important. If He was not raised from the dead there would be no miracle available for you Justine, but He was resurrected and the apostles gave witness to His resurrection with great power. So when you are healed God is going to prove through your miracle that Jesus was raised from the dead. It is a witness to His resurrection...do you understand?"

I went on to say, "Before we pray I want you to know that I am going to pray against your belief systems that say to you that you are incurable, you have to live with this arthritis and that you are damaged goods. Next we are going to take authority over demonic spirits, like a spirit of infirmity- Jesus rebuked spirits of infirmity all the time- and we will come against spirits that have tormented you with depression. Do you understand Justine?"

She said she did so I said "are you ready to pray?" She said that she was ready.

I opened the bottle of oil and poured some on Justine's head. Then I handed her the bottle so she could smell the oil and then we let her friend smell it. They enjoyed smelling it. Then we prayed and thanked God for His power to give witness to the resurrection of Jesus Christ. We then commanded spirits of infirmity and tormenting spirits to cease their operations against her and prayed against hopelessness. We commanded the arthritis to evacuate her body.

When we finished Justine said, "This is really weird. My leg fells like pins and needles all over it." I said it is because the arthritis is gone now and the nerves effected by it are free and are coming to life again as your system is adjusting to the miracle you received. I told her to give me her cane and told her to start walking. She took four or five awkward steps and turned with amazement. She said, "My leg feels weak but I can walk." "Of course it is weak," I said, "you have been walking with a cane and your muscles need rebuilding. Then I prayed, "I command strength to come into your leg right now in Jesus name, so you don't have to use a cane ever again." She said "I don't want to use a cane anymore…I want to walk." So she took off across the parking lot walking without her cane. Thank you Father!

Well we spent the next few minutes hugging one another and rejoicing at how God had shown His love to Justine we hugged some more and then said our goodbyes.

We all have the ability to count upon the power of God so that we can give witness to the resurrection of Jesus Christ. I know it says that it was the apostles doing it in this case, but it does not mean that only apostles can give witness to the resurrection by using the power of God; we all are called to do so. We all have the potential to perform miracles in the name of Jesus when we understand that Jesus has risen from the dead and has given us direct access to *great grace* just as it was for the apostles. Opps I stand corrected, **"great grace was upon them all," not just the apostles. Praise God.**

Wouldn't it be nice if we all took our position as **witnesses to the resurrection of Jesus Christ**, knowing that power is available to us to get the job done? When we break the mind-sets that say that something is impossible, look what happens. We dealt with everything that was stopping Justine from walking without a cane. Everyone who is oppressed of the devil is fair game for us. We can do miracles, when we use the power of God to give witness to the resurrection of Jesus. Get used to the idea that you too can do miracles, because that is what all believers in Christ do. We do miracles! It's what we do.

WITNESSES ARE MEANT TO CARRY THE POWER OF GOD.

> But *ye shall receive power*, after that the Holy Ghost is come upon you: and *ye shall be witnesses unto me* both in Jerusalem, and in all Judaea, and in Samaria, and unto the uttermost part of the earth (Acts 1:8, italics mine).

Again, witnesses receive power after that the Holy Ghost is come upon them. The Holy Ghost brings the power. The power resident within you enables you to give powerful witness to the resurrection of Jesus Christ. If you are willing to be His witness, the power for you to give witness is yours. How would you like to miraculously heal someone who is a cripple? It is easy when you have received power when the Holy Ghost came upon you.

I believe many of you will take this revelation and run with it. I believe some will become so powerful that whole communities will take note that the same power that raised Jesus from the dead is in you and is shaking the powers of darkness that hold people in the bondage of hopelessness. I know you will be one of them. Do it for them Father, in Jesus Name.

No Shortage of Power

For he whom God hath sent speaketh the words of God: for God giveth not the Spirit by measure unto him (John 3:34).

In Johannesburg, South Africa, there is a young apostle named Macphilips Jasper. Macphilips is from Nigeria and grew up in a Muslim family. When he was a young teenager he heard the gospel for the first time. Macphilips responded to the invitation of life through Christ Jesus. To his Muslim family, this was a source of embarrassment and Macphilips was rejected. But in heaven he was accepted in the beloved gaining the favor and inheritance of a son. Macphilips had a burning desire to get involved in Bible studies and sensed the call of the Spirit to preach the word of God. At the age of 17 Macphilips had already been preaching for a while, but he decided to go into the ministry full time.

From that day until this one he has preached in over 29 nations of the world. He returned from Korea in 2012, has flown millions of miles and has led countless people to the Lord. While he travels, his wife Mercy, raises their four children from their base in South Africa.

I met Macphilips on a mission trip to his native Nigeria. I heard him preach and he instantly became my favorite preacher. He is so vibrant and on fire and extremely dynamic. Macphilips loves people. He will do anything to go where Jesus calls him and to preach the gospel of the kingdom. He is tried and true. He has been tested. He has not been found wanting.

In 2008 MacPhilips asked me to come to South Africa to minister with him and to pray for him. I agreed but I would have to wait a couple of years to go. In 2010 I went to Johannesburg and stayed for two weeks with Macphilips and his delightful family. After two years in prayer the stage was finally set. God had been dealing with me about the scriptures where Jesus "healed them all."

> But when Jesus knew it, he withdrew himself from thence: and great multitudes followed him, and *he healed them all* (Matthew 12:15, italics mine).

> Now when the sun was setting, all they that had any sick with divers diseases brought them unto him; and he laid his hands *on every one of them*, and healed them (Luke 4:40, italics mine).

> And the whole multitude sought to touch him: *for there went virtue out of him, and healed them all* (Luke 6:19, italics mine).

I was not satisfied with healing just a few people. If my Lord healed them all, I must be missing something if I was not getting the same results as He. When I am pressing into the kingdom for an answer, I keep praying in tongues and kept speaking the scriptures that pertain to what I am seeking for. In this case I saw that Jesus healed them all. As I spent time with Macphilips, I kept telling him that Jesus heals them all. He was always very quick to agree with me and to echo that reality back to me every time I said it, preached about it, or declared that we would heal them all, just like Jesus did.

Our fellowship revolved around that reality: a reality that has its origins in the heart of our God and the Father of our

Lord Jesus Christ. We kept saying to one another that Jesus heals them all. It was great to hear Macphilips pick up the intercessory beat of my heart and join me in vocalizing the heart of God for the people of South Africa. After all hadn't we prayed for two years that God would do something very special? So this was our chance to see it come to pass.

In the black populations of Johannesburg's townships sickness and great poverty plague the people. HIV is reported to be at 25% in these communities. On our second night together we went to a church that met in a tent. Macphilips had gone door-to-door preaching and praying for people in this community until they had formed a small church and developed a pastor. It was an honor to minister in a church that was the fruit of his labors.

I greeted the people by speaking of the relationship I have with Macphilips and how this night had been two years in the making and two years of praying for God to bring it to pass. I talked about obedience to God, how Macphilips had been obedient to come to South Africa, and how their church was established through his obedience to God.

I told them that I had been called to heal the sick. I recognized the call to heal through what interested me most about Jesus and what He had to say about it. I spoke of how He required obedience on my part, to pray for the sick, to establish me in my calling to heal the sick. But the call is not fully set or proven without putting the call into action. Sincere effort is required. Thinking about it does not lead to action without a commitment to be obedient to the heavenly calling. I testified of the times that I had obeyed God and prayed for the sick, laying hands upon them and speaking the scriptures over them. I told them that I had not felt at all confident and was fearful in these earlier days of obedience, but God kept encouraging me and leading me more and more to obey.

One time I prayed and said to God that I lacked the courage to do what He had called me to do. He said to me, "Have

I not told you to be strong and very courageous? Get up and go do it for I am with you." I immediately got up and went into the hospital praying for everyone. The word He spoke to me gave me faith, and boldness came over me, and approaching the sick became very easy. The key for me was that God said I am with you.

> How God anointed Jesus of Nazareth with the Holy Ghost and with power: who went about doing good, and healing all that were oppressed of the devil; for *God was with him* (Acts 10:38, italics mine).

God was with Jesus, He anointed Him with the Holy Ghost and with power, which enabled Him to do good and to heal ALL! The anointing upon Him **healed all**. *Just like the Father was with Jesus - He was with me.* God was with me. He came with me to South Africa, the Holy Spirit brooding over me, influencing my meditations and imagination. I was pregnant with promise, full of the Holy Ghost and power.

While speaking in the tent that night, I realized that God had been with me *since that day in the hospital when I prayed for the sick,* never leaving me, and always going with me into every encounter with His word and His Spirit. I never go alone, and neither do you. He is always watching over His word to perform it. When you speak the words of God His Spirit is available "without measure" to bring about salvation and deliverance. The revelation that He is with me, attending to the ministry He had begun in me, mentoring me by His Spirit, and empowering me as I speak for Him, **brought manifestations of real freedom**. I was in Him and He was in me. He walks in me and talks in me. He is my God and I am His child. He deeply loves me and completely accepts me. He father's me with His truth and instruction. When I am in agreement with

Him and speak what He puts on my heart, His Spirit is available without measure.

Out of the 100 people in attendance that night, 30 of them needed healing. That night 30 of them came forth for prayer and 30 out of the 30 left the tent completely healed. Jesus used me to heal them all. I took part in the realm of Glory. I had been holding onto this realm by faith and confessing it as the reality it truly is, until it manifested in an atmosphere of faith. This is only one example of "all being healed." When you are certain that Jesus has all authority in heaven and earth, confidence comes in the reality of the kingdom. You realize that because He could not fail, you cannot fail. There is no shortage of His power in you.

10
CAPTAINS OF THOUSANDS

We gaze with anticipation to those things which will
shortly come to pass. The timetables of God are syn-
chronized and the entire host of heaven awaits the "end time
harvest." As we peer into the war room we see battle plans for
our day. We are going into labor and are crowning at the pre-
cise time when Zion will PUSH; bringing forth the greatest
harvest of souls ever to be witnessed on the earth. This prolific
bringing forth will captivate the attention of the entire earth as
billions are regenerated and sowers over take reapers.

I hope you will understand that God is looking for captains
who will be able to serve thousands, training and equipping
them for the work ahead. Why not step up today and ask the
Lord to prepare you?

There are plenty of reasons to believe you are not qualified.
When David was hiding out in a cave from King Saul, men
came to him from all over to join him in battle. Most of them
had suffered greatly and were in bad shape.

> And every one *that was* in distress, and every
> one that *was* in debt, and every one *that was* dis-
> contented, gathered themselves unto him; and
> he became a captain over them: and there were
> with him about four hundred men (1 Samuel
> 22:2).

David became captain over 400 men. Everyone that was in distress, or in debt or discontented gathered unto him. They wanted to be a part of something greater than themselves. I encounter such brothers and sisters all the time.

Don't you want to be part of something greater than your recent troubles and discontents? With this beginning, David's army grew as did these men. They became mighty men and captains over hundreds and captains over thousands. God has a placement for you. Separate yourself unto this purpose. There are mighty exploits ahead for you as you defeat giants and deliver those held in bondage. In our day we have an advantage that these men did not. Our enemies are not people, but are demonic powers that have already been defeated by Jesus Christ. In His name we are able to take the land.

11
HEAVEN'S BEACH HEAD

So what is a beach·head? [n].

1. A position on an enemy shoreline captured by troops in advance of an invading force.

2. A first achievement that opens the way for further developments; a foothold:

Heaven is invading the earth. All around us we see the signs of shaking. Satan and his demons who accuse us before God day and night are being displaced from heavenly realms. They are being cast out into the earth. The downward thrust of heaven's invading forces is slamming Satan and his demons to the earth. We are the troops on the ground capturing positions on the enemy's shoreline. Our achievements open the way for further kingdom developments. We are God's foothold. As we work in tandem with the hosts of heaven a position being firmly established with kingdom skillsets. We are part of the kingdom that cannot be moved. In the war rooms of heaven our victory over darkness has been laid out. Our victory is certain. We are part of the new creation that cannot be shaken.

> And there was war in heaven: Michael and his angels fought against the dragon; and the dragon fought and his angels, And prevailed not; neither was their place found any more in heaven. And the great dragon was cast out, that old serpent, called the Devil, and Satan, which deceiveth the whole world: he was cast out into the earth, and his angels were cast out with him. And I heard a loud voice saying in heaven, Now is come salvation, and strength, and the kingdom of our God, and the power of his Christ: for the accuser of our brethren is cast down, which accused them before our God day and night (Revelation 12:7–10).

Do not confuse this with what Jesus said about the initial rebellion of Satan and a third of the angels.

> And the seventy returned again with joy, saying, Lord, even the devils are subject unto us through thy name. And he said unto them, I beheld Satan as lightning fall from heaven. Behold, I give unto you power to tread on serpents and scorpions, and over all the power of the enemy: and nothing shall by any means hurt you. Notwithstanding in this rejoice not, that the spirits are subject unto you; but rather rejoice, because your names are written in heaven (Luke 10:17–20).

What Jesus said in Luke already took place, but what came to John in the Book of Revelation was yet to *come to pass*; it was a revelation of the future.

> The Revelation of Jesus Christ, which God gave unto him, to shew unto his servants things which *must shortly come to pass*; and he sent and signified it by his angel unto his servant John: Who bare record of the word of God, and of the testimony of Jesus Christ, and of all things that he saw (Revelation 1:1–2, italics mine).

The downward pressure of this battle is creating chaos, war always does. There are signs in the heavens and in the earth beneath. The whole creation is groaning. The people of the earth are in fear because of all the shaking. Governments and economies are rattled, people are afraid all over the world. Nuclear threats, terrorism, famines, earthquakes, etc. nothing escapes the shaking, except for that which cannot be shaken.

> Men's hearts failing them for fear, and for looking after those things which are coming on the earth: for the powers of heaven shall be shaken (Luke 21:26).

> Whose voice then shook the earth: but now he hath promised, saying, Yet once more I shake not the earth only, but also heaven. And this word, Yet once more, signifieth the removing of those things that are shaken, as of things that are made, that those things which cannot be shaken may remain. Wherefore we receiving a kingdom which cannot be moved, let us have grace, whereby we may serve God acceptably with reverence and godly fear: For our God is a consuming fire (Hebrews 12:26–29).

The shaking is not new to the earth. God's voice shook the earth in the days of Moses. The earth is being shaken again, but this time the heavens are also shaking. The demonic riffraff are being displaced from the heavens. The pressure of that warfare is being felt everywhere in the heavens and in the earth.

Satan realizes that his time is short so he has come down with great wrath. He and his demons are fighting the people of earth in an effort to defy God and His creation. He comes to steal, kill and to destroy. Governments are attempting to legislate us because of economic pressure, with the same failed ideas and strategies that have insanely driven us towards financial collapse.

My question to the people of the earth is "have you not identified your real enemy?" Satan is on the offensive warring against the people of the earth and is being assaulted by the angelic forces who are doing the will of God. God is doing the shaking, but God is not your enemy. He is shaking things up and shaking out all those things that can be shaken. **At the end of this shaking, what you have is not the survival of the fittest, but the survival of the faithful.** May God purge from us anything that would limit us from obtaining our full inheritance.

Those who have received and are stewarding heaven's invasion get stronger each day, not weaker. They are also displacing the enemy. Here on the earth believers are bringing the powers of the age to come into their sphere of influence and setting people free. The kingdom of heaven is being actualized by their prayers and mighty acts. Instead of being shaken and rattled, we are being *refreshed* in the battle and strengthened by the power of His might. We get stronger JUST like carbon hardens to form a diamond. Our brightness becomes clearer and stronger. Anytime it gets dark around us we shine brighter and displace demonic powers within our jurisdictional authority. By walking close to Jesus we can make a huge impact around us all the time. We are heaven's beach head.

In the arena of our assignments intercession and the acts of the saints are making a difference in the kingdoms of this world. We are causing people to understand the big picture. What is happening is not evolving from the temporal visible realm that most have focused upon, but from the eternal, invisible realm. The warfare and the shaking of the temporal originates from the unseen realm.

Satan is being cast out of the heavens, but it is no easier for him when he encounters the sons and daughters of God on the earth. He is taking a beating from both the angelic forces driving him from the heavens and from the sons and daughters of God who have the Greater One on the inside of them. We are battle-hardened against the real enemy, but are gentle and dove-like towards the children of men. We have the big picture.

THE BIG PICTURE

Satan is cast out and has come down so that the saints of God will overcome him, and not be overcome by him.

> And I heard a loud voice saying in heaven, *Now is come salvation, and strength, and the kingdom of our God, and the power of his Christ*: for the accuser of our brethren is cast down, which accused them before our God day and night. And they overcame him by the blood of the Lamb, and by the word of their testimony; and they loved not their lives unto the death (Revelation 12:10–11, italics mine).

He is thrust down so that we can whip him in this realm. He is bread for us. This day your enemies turn their backs and flee. God has confidence in us. The least of us is greater than John the Baptist. We can whip the devil. We are called to do so. We overcome him by the blood of the Lamb and by the word of our testimony and by not loving the world and the things that are in it. We love the people and hold forth the word of life. Our gospel is not hidden, but the oracles of God are released from our mouths quickening the measure of faith in every man to believe, converting the sinner from the error of his way and lovingly guiding them back into the glorious liberty they have been called to.

> And when the dragon saw that he was cast unto the earth, *he persecuted the woman which brought forth the man child*. And to the woman were given two wings of a great eagle, that she might fly into the wilderness, into her place, where she is nourished for a time, and times, and half a time, from the face of the serpent. And the serpent cast out of his mouth water as a flood after the woman, that he might cause her to be carried away of the flood. And the earth helped the woman, and the earth opened her mouth, and swallowed up the flood which the dragon cast out of his mouth. And the dragon was wroth with the woman, and went to make war with the remnant of her seed, *which keep the commandments of God, and have the testimony of Jesus Christ* (Revelation 12:13–17, italics mine).

We are the *woman* that is bringing forth the man child. Our role is to birth sons and daughters of God. It matters not that we have an enemy. The earth is not very fond of Satan either and has a part to play in helping us.

> Who hath heard such a thing? who hath seen such things? Shall the earth be made to bring forth in one day? *or* shall a nation be born at once? for as soon as Zion travailed, she brought forth her children (Isaiah 66:8).

The warfare we experience is against the enemies of the plan of God. His plan involves His desire that all men might be saved.

> I exhort therefore, that, first of all, *supplications, prayers, intercessions, and giving of thanks, be made for all men*; For kings, and *for* all that are in authority; that we may lead a quiet and peaceable life in all godliness and honesty. For this *is* good and acceptable in the sight of God our Saviour; *Who will have all men to be saved*, and to come unto the knowledge of the truth. For *there is* one God, and one mediator between God and men, the man Christ Jesus (1 Timothy 2:1–5, italics mine).

Through intercession of the saints we are co-laboring with the plan of God that all men might be saved. Our warfare is against demonic forces. Men are not the enemy, Satan is. When we realize that people are valuable to God we see all men as precious in His sight and the demonic forces as "the enemy." We rightly challenge God's enemies when we seek to bring forth seed unto God.

As heaven invades the earth we become heaven's beachhead. Heaven's forces invade the earth through the inner man because of the kingdom of God within us. We are the ones who keep the commandments of God and have the testimony of Jesus Christ. When we are fully awake and purposefully pursuing our role in birthing sons and daughters, Satan comes forth to make war against us. I say "So What? Why should I be afraid of a foe who is already defeated?" **My picture hangs in Satan's post office just like the F.B.I.'s Ten Most Wanted fugitives list.** From where I sit Satan is already defeated.

Behold, I give unto you power to tread on ser-
pents and scorpions, and over all the power
of the enemy: and nothing shall by any means
hurt you (Luke 10:19).

When you possess God's power over all the power of the
enemy, you get stronger in battle and you keep having victory
after victory. You shine brighter and brighter. Just as carbon
under pressure becomes a diamond, you become more and
more capable and competent as you grow in the grace of our
Lord Jesus Christ. When your resolve to remain in the battle
with all the saints you become *relentless.* Uriah the Hittite had
this resolve.

And when Uriah was come unto him, David
demanded *of him* how Joab did, and how the
people did, and how the war prospered. And
David said to Uriah, Go down to thy house, and
wash thy feet. And Uriah departed out of the
king's house, and there followed him a mess
of meat from the king. But Uriah slept at the
door of the king's house with all the servants
of his lord, and went not down to his house.
And when they had told David, saying, Uriah
went not down unto his house, David said unto
Uriah, Camest thou not from *thy* journey? why
then didst thou not go down unto thine house?
And Uriah said unto David, *The ark, and Israel,
and Judah, abide in tents; and my lord Joab, and the
servants of my lord, are encamped in the open fields;
shall I then go into mine house, to eat and to drink,
and to lie with my wife? as thou livest, and as thy soul
liveth, I will not do this thing* (2 Samuel 11:7–11,
italics mine).

The more you require His grace, in any area of weakness, the more it abounds. Every encounter brings more strength. At the end of your race you who overcome, and remain faithful to the end, will rule over nations. Not a bad deal.

> And he that overcometh, and keepeth my works unto the end, to him will I give power over the nations (Revelation 2:26).

You do not work alone. The whole family in heaven and in earth forms a partnership in your kingdom pursuits. The prayers of the saints prayed from the beginning of time unto the present join with our prayers. **There is no expiration date for prayers prayed in the past. The saints of old have seen our day through revelation and have prayed for us.**

Add to that the present ministry of Jesus Christ; the greatest intercessor of all…

> Hath in these last days spoken unto us by *his* Son, whom he hath appointed *heir of all things,* by whom also he made the worlds; Who being the brightness of *his* glory, and the express image of his person, and *upholding all things by the word of his power, when he had by himself purged our sins, sat down on the right hand of the Majesty on high* (Hebrews 1:1–3, italics mine).

Currently He upholds all things by the word of His power. This is not past tense. And He also prays for you. Jesus has a standing in God that no human has. He is the High Priest over the house of God. His prayers are answered.

> By so much was Jesus made a *surety of a better testament.* And they truly were many priests, because they were not suffered to continue by reason of death: But this *man, because he continu-*

eth ever, hath an *unchangeable priesthood*. Wherefore he is able also to save them to the uttermost that come unto God by him, seeing *he ever liveth to make intercession for them* (Hebrews 7:21–25, italics mine).

Suretyship, n. [from *surety*] The state of being surety; *the obligation of a person to answer for another*, and make good any debt or loss which may occur from another's delinquency.

Jesus prayers make up any deficiency. He stands in the gap for you as you align yourself to His will.

Our prayers, when aligned with heaven's purposes, make us the most powerful generation to have ever walked the earth. You were born into this prophetic hour and you have what it takes in your new nature to rule and reign with Christ in this temporal life. To do so with excellence and remaining focused on the plan is the highest pathway of all.

Angelic forces join us in our battles and also protect us. Jesus is the Captain of the host, the God of the angelic armies who surround the saints with multitudes of angels. The more angels you require the more that are assigned to you. Take the battle to the gate and everything required to win is yours in Christ.

> But ye are come unto mount Sion, and unto the city of the living God, the heavenly Jerusalem, and *to an innumerable company of angels* (Hebrews 12:22, italics mine)

All of the resources of heaven are at our disposal. Jesus is hungry for us to receive and to activate the full inheritance we have been given. When we do we become uncontrollable to Satan and his forces. We become unstoppable. I wish everyone, including myself, would awake out of sleep and rise up in the revelation we have been given in Christ. The Holy Spirit's job is to make us aware of it. He is unable to do so if we are dull of hearing or totally ignorant of the *availability of His counsel.*

You are God's authority in the earthly realm. If you don't answer the call you are just swept away in the waves of delusion. To forfeit the call of God is the enemy's gain; but tragically it is your loss, and a loss to all of us. To opt out of the plan is to do more harm than good.

He that is not with me is against me: and he that gathereth not with me scattereth (Luke 11:23).

To be neutral is to choose sides against Jesus. I know that's not our intent, but it becomes the default result for those who do not do the works of Christ. Not working with Him is to work against him. He has called us to work towards the end that *all men might be saved.* They go unsaved if we don't overcome the devil in our lives. When we have no testimony of Christ and do not keep His commandments how can we overcome?

You might have a great list of reasons why you feel unqualified or inadequate, but when you walk in the spirit, those excuses fall away. The Holy Spirit can get you past everything stopping you.

You might ask "how do I do this?"

Just start today and ask the Holy Spirit to guide you. As you read His word ask Him to show you something you can do today. Stay in His word until you see it. As you go about your day, trust Him to alert you when opportunity appears.

He will give you assignments that, when you do them, help you gain experience in hearing and doing. If you will actively continue this daily, you will be surprised at how effective you will become. Over time your story will change. What you once found really hard to do will become easy. Your whole life becomes different because you have overcome Satan through the process. Praise God.

The first time I spoke to someone about Jesus I was intimidated. I fumbled through the experience. By my standard I did not do very well, but in heaven the angels were breathless. In heaven they were at attention watching as someone stepped out in faith for the first time, like a baby trying to walk for the first time. From heaven's point of view I was a hero, but in my own eyes I felt as if I had failed.

The more I tried to share the gospel the better I got. Isn't that the way it is in most anything? You may feel uneasy at first, but hang in there because you can and will get better. God began to teach me better ways to minister the Truth as I was faithful to try what He was giving me. The same will be true for you.

With all that has been said, my hope is that you will get excited to do in your own life not only what has been taught but also explore for yourself the mysteries of God. He has secrets to share with you. Secrets that will come as you are busy doing what he has called you to do. Keep building yourselves up on your most holy faith and believe with Jesus that you to are able to do the works He did and greater. So as you take it from here, May God amply bless you with every blessing and multiply his grace to you. God Speed!

THE END

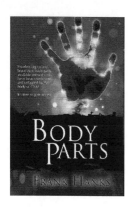

Other titles from Frank Hanks include:

BODY PARTS

HOW TO GET KICKED OUT OF CHURCH

The Author is open to publishers wishing to translate and or acquire distribution rights internationally. Agents welcome

Order any of Frank's books by the case for Bible studies:

- 25 books per case
- More than 10 cases = $8.00 per book + shipping and handling
- Prices for books going to missions organizations are favorably negotiable at any quantity

Order books direct from: Empty Hospitals Publishing:

E-mail: emptyhospitals@gmail.com.
Website: www.emptyhospitals.org

Mailing Address:
Empty Hospitals Publishing
PO Box 28013 Highland Green
Red Deer, AB. T4N 7C2
Canada

Ministry Information:

Contact Frank Hanks and his ministry about speaking in mass harvest campaigns, conferences, revival meetings or to receive more information about his ministry:

E-mail: emptyhospitals@gmail.com.
Website: www.emptyhospitals.org

Mailing Address:
Empty Hospitals International
PO Box 28013 Highland Green
Red Deer, AB. T4N 7C2
Canada

Made in the USA
Middletown, DE
05 April 2015